ROADBLOCKS
TO RECEIVING:

WHAT GOD HAS TO SAY ABOUT IT

by
Dr. Lloyd Hudson

Roadblocks to Receiving:
What God Has to Say About It
ISBN 0-88144-294-1
Copyright © 2008 by Dr. Lloyd Hudson

Published by
Victory Publishing
P. O. Box 701434
Tulsa, OK 74170

Dedication

To Jamie, whose price is far above rubies.

Contents

Foreword ....

    Chapter 1 It's More Than Lack of Faith.......................................

    Chapter 2 Seek Ye First the Kingdom of God ....

    Chapter 3 In Vain They Worship Me ....

    Chapter 4 Repent and Do the First Works...................................

    Chapter 5 Walk Not in the Counsel of the Ungodly ....

    Chapter 6 Spiritual Growth:
                 We Should No Longer be Children ....

    Chapter 7 Effective Prayer: May the Word Abide in You.............

    Chapter 8 Love Your Neighbor as Yourself ....

    Chapter 9 Get Out of the Past ....

  Chapter 10 Worry and Fear: Destroyers of Faith ....

About the Author ....

FOREWORD

Years ago I made a firm decision to begin to base my belief system on the Word of God. I grew weary of listening to the advice and opinions of well-meaning co-workers, friends, talk show hosts, movie stars, university professors, and counselors. I simply decided once and for all to seek the advice of the King of kings and the Lord of lords about...*stuff.* My first impulse when faced with a decision of great or small importance is now, "What does God have to say about it?" For any issue, question, or problem, I now seek the recommendation of Almighty God.

Although this sounds quite complex at first, it really is not. God's counsel on everything pertaining to life is found in His holy written Word. Reading the Bible as God's infallible, inerrant Word is like God speaking directly to me. No, on the contrary, basing my belief system on the Bible was really a *life-simplifying* decision. No more trying to figure everything out on my own or stressing myself out about "life-changing" decisions. Seeking God's counsel through His Word...what a novel idea! I only wish I had thought of it before I was well into my thirties!!

This book, as well as the others in the "What God Has to Say About It" series, is based on the authority of holy Scripture alone. Every effort has been made in these books to lessen the opinions, biases, and speculations of man and to heighten the Truth revealed in God's Word. Of course, I cannot claim that this book itself is inspired by God; however, the Scripture references contained in the book are indeed "God-breathed," and this should give credence to the content.

CHAPTER 1

IT'S MORE THAN LACK OF FAITH

One of the most intriguing questions in the Church today is, "Why do some Christians fail to receive from God?" Why do the answers to prayer manifest for some people and not for others? Why are God's promises showing up in some people's lives and not in others? Why do some strong Christian men and women fail to receive their healing? Why do some believers never receive their deliverance from bondages? Why do many members of the Body of Christ continue to live in fear? Why do so many of us suffer long-term depression and fail to see peace manifest in our lives? Why do many of us continue to have lifelong financial struggles despite believing scriptures on prosperity? Why, why, why? Why do people of the Church, especially many of us here in the United States, fail to see God's promises come true in our lives? What forces are out there that are robbing countless Christian believers of their rights and privileges in Christ?

The age-old answer has been "a lack of faith." I think that is definitely true in part, as the Bible tells us that indeed we do receive all the promises of God through faith. But I have seen people who appear to sincerely believe and stand strong in faith, and yet fail to receive. I have experienced this in my own faith walk as well. No, there must be more involved than lack of faith. There must be. There must be some other hindrances out there that the Church is falling prey to, and we need to know about them.

I would like to know. I would like to know so much that I decided to see what God has to say about it. After all, who better to provide us insight to this perplexing question than the Creator of the Universe Himself? So I began to pray for the spirit of wisdom and revelation in the knowledge of Him, and I began to seek, and I began to knock. And as usual, God provided me answers in the most normal and unspectacular fashion through His Word. As usual, God's Word sheds light on the subject, and since I base my belief system on the Word of God, it was easy for me to believe these truths.

Obviously, I am not claiming to have all the answers, and I am certainly not prepared to give everyone who reads this a personal explanation for their individual situation. I am merely putting together some of the divine knowledge that God has shared with us through His holy written Word. I am talking about things that God has told us that keep us from receiving. I am talking about ROADBLOCKS TO RECEIVING.

Now, please don't get me wrong. Don't misunderstand me. I am NOT talking about why problems in life occur or why "bad things happen to good people." It is very clear through studying the Bible that "many are the afflictions of the righteous." The mountains will present themselves. The trials in life will come to all. The icebergs will be present. What we are going to study is what God has to say about the ability of some of us to navigate through the icebergs of life, while others seemingly cannot. Why some Christians appear to receive from God and others struggle. I want to discuss what the Bible has to say about roadblocks to receiving.

Why even talk about roadblocks to receiving what belongs to us through Christ Jesus? For one thing, many of us may not have identified certain things in our lives, our spiritual walk, our prayer lives, etc. that have actually been hindering us from receiving our blessings. Many of us have been living beneath our rights and privileges as children of God because we have not identified these roadblocks. There are things we can do and cannot do, choices that we make and don't make, that actually can hinder our faith and answered prayer. God told us about them, wrote them down for us, and He absolutely wants us to know about them, because He is a God of love. He wants to shower us with His blessings, just as any parent wants to do with their child.

Many Christians simply want to know why they are not seeing things manifest in their lives that they are believing in faith for God to provide. Many Christians read God's Word, believe God's Word, and stand on certain scriptures in faith, yet fail to see the manifestation in their lives.

Some of us believe that Jesus is our Healer (1 Peter 2:24), but we don't receive our healing.

Some of us believe Jesus was beaten for our peace (Isaiah 53:5, the chastisement of our peace was upon Him), yet we continue to live in turmoil.

Some of us believe that we have been delivered from the powers of darkness (Colossians 1:13), yet we continue to struggle with a bondage.

Some of us believe in divine protection (Psalm 91), yet death and disaster seem to be ever present.

Some of us believe that God will supply all of our needs according to His riches in glory by Christ Jesus (Philippians 4:19), but we continually live in a state of financial crisis.

For some of us, nothing ever seems to get better in certain areas of our lives, despite an enormous amount of belief in the Word of God.

What's up? Why is this so? What are the roadblocks in our lives that are preventing us from getting from point A to point B?

If I were to tell you to go to Oklahoma City from Tulsa, you would be able to get in your car, turn the ignition, get on the turnpike, and make your way there. No problem. Just put gas in your car, get your toll money ready, and it is a very straightforward task. But what if on the way, on the turnpike, you run into a roadblock? What if a fog settles in, and you can no longer see where you are going? What if there is a major wreck on the highway that has blocked both lanes and there are no exits in sight? What if there is a detour sign that does nothing but lead you astray or get you lost? What if a storm (in life) comes up, a level 5 tornado approaches, and makes the way seem virtually impassable? What if darkness falls, and one or both headlights are out? What if you run across a roadblock in life, and all of sudden the seemingly simple task of getting from Tulsa to Oklahoma City appears impossible? What are you going to do?

If we can find out what God has to say about these roadblocks and what He has to say about overcoming them, then it will certainly be an advantage to us.

We are going to find out what God has to say about some roadblocks to receiving His blessings. As we go through these, make an attempt to identify one or more roadblocks that may exist in your life. Applying God's Word, being a doer of God's Word and not just a hearer only, is what will change lives and allow abundant life to manifest.

CHAPTER 2

SEEK YE FIRST THE KINGDOM OF GOD

Matthew 6:33

But SEEK YE FIRST THE KINGDOM of God, and his righteousness; and all these things shall be added unto you.

One problem, one major roadblock, to receiving the blessings of God through Christ that I believe is extremely prevalent in the Church, and especially here in the United States, is the Word we are learning is not falling on good soil. It can't produce in our lives because we are seeking first the things instead of seeking first the Kingdom. We are seeking to fill our voids with "things" instead of filling the void with God, who is the only person who can satisfy such a void—a sense that something is missing, a dissatisfaction in life.

Remember, Jesus said that we are to seek FIRST the Kingdom of God and His righteousness, and THEN all the things will be added unto us. Not seek first the THINGS that we think are missing from our lives, which is what we often do. Seek ye FIRST the Kingdom. Seek ye FIRST the Kingdom.

A void means that something is missing. But it doesn't just mean a space where something is missing, but that something is so yearned for, so desired, that if not there, a craving will exist to fill it, and a feeling of being incomplete or being unfulfilled will be present without it.

What are some of the things that people try to fill this spiritual void with—this dissatisfaction in life, this sense that something is missing?

Money and Possessions—people who always seem to be buying something new and exciting to keep them happy, filling their void with the pursuit of money and possessions.

Fame—the quest for recognition among peers, a driving force in the lives of some.

Food—people turning to food as their main source of comfort.

Relationships—people who seem to always be moving from relationship to relationship to relationship, seeking fulfillment in life through another person. These are the same people whose happiness, sadness, or whatever emotion is always based and dependent on their relationships. When there is more sadness than happiness, then it is time to find a new relationship, because that MUST be the problem. Their lives go up...and down...according to the status of their relationships.

Drugs/Alcohol—since these chemicals can temporarily and artificially ease the pain in life, they are often sought as a means to fill a void—a sense of something missing in life.

Pornography—a bondage that some people turn to.

Sexual Fulfillment—those who are ONLY happy if they are constantly being SEXUALLY FULFILLED. No happiness, no joy, if no sex.

Children—I see this all the time at work. CHILD WORSHIP. The child is taking the #1 place in your life that belongs to God. Child worship is a perverted form of love. Your child should NOT be the most important thing in your life. God reserved that spot when He created us for Him, and if we attempt to fill it with anything else, and that includes our children, then a void will exist. The effects on the child, by the way, are devastating. I see young men in their twenties and thirties who are still totally dependent on their mother and have no idea how to function in life, because their mother never gave them a chance.

Work—people who drown themselves in their work, and then don't have to face the issues of life, because they are always devoted to their work or their career.

Church—filling a spiritual void with church and outward religion instead of developing an intimate relationship with the Father. A void is present because God isn't.

Friendships—people whose primary effort is to see how many friends they can have. Why? Because there is a dissatisfaction, a sense that something is missing, and they think that having more friends will quench the thirst, but it won't.

The ONLY thing that will permanently and satisfactorily fill our spiritual voids, our sense that something is missing in our lives, the sense that there must be something more, the sense that full and genuine happiness won't occur without is God, knowing and establishing a relationship with God through His Gift, Jesus Christ.

Jesus said that we can't serve two masters, for if we try we will end up loving one and hating the other.

Matthew 6:24

NO ONE CAN SERVE TWO MASTERS. For you will hate one and love the other, or be devoted to one and despise the other. You cannot serve both God and money. (NLT)

Have you ever wondered why almost all lottery winners' lives take a turn for the worse

afterwards? Statistics are staggering. After they win an enormous amount of money, they attempt to fill spiritual voids with "things," when what they are really missing is a relationship with God,

You see, if we don't seek first the Kingdom, or seek first the completing of ourselves with our relationship with God through Jesus, the void doesn't get filled. The feeling of dissatisfaction remains. The void is present because God isn't. RESTORATION never seems to happen. Nothing can satisfy a spiritual void, if it exists, besides God. Nothing!

It is simply impossible to fill a space in your life that is meant and reserved for God, by God our Creator, with anything but God!!!! It simply won't work. It would be like trying to fill your car tank up with kerosene instead of gasoline. Your car is designed for unleaded gasoline, not kerosene or any other type of fossil fuel. It simply won't work. It would be like trying to breathe carbon dioxide instead of oxygen. It simply will not work. It would be like filling an empty swimming pool with sand! It might look good, but it is simply not going to work! The void is there, because God isn't!

Jesus put it this way in the Parable of the Sower. Remember, we are talking about roadblocks to receiving; roadblocks to producing a crop in our lives—and here we are talking about the roadblock of SEEKING FIRST THINGS in life instead of seeking first God's Kingdom.

Matthew 13:3-8

A farmer went out to plant some seed. As he scattered it across his field, some seeds fell on a FOOTPATH, and the birds came and ate them. Other seeds fell on SHALLOW SOIL with underlying rock. The plants sprang up quickly, but they soon wilted beneath the hot sun and died because the roots had no nourishment in the shallow soil. Other seeds fell among THORNS that shot up and choked out the tender blades. But some seeds fell on FERTILE SOIL and produced a crop that was thirty, sixty, and even a hundred times as much as had been planted. (NLT)

You see, we all want to produce a crop in our life.

We want healing.

We want peace.

We want deliverance.

We want financial blessings and financial security.

We want divine protection.

But our soil may not be fertile. It may not be good ground at this point in our lives because we are not SEEKING FIRST THE KINGDOM.

Then Jesus Himself explains the parable to the disciples, probably because it is such an important message.

Matthew 13:19-23

The seed that fell on the hard path represents those who hear the Good News about the Kingdom and don't understand it. Then the evil one comes and snatches the seed away from their hearts. [These are people who are not born again and thus the message of the cross is foolishness to them, they cannot understand it. [For the message of the cross is foolishness to those who are perishing, but to us who are being saved it is the power of God. (1 Corinthians 1:18 NKJV)]

The rocky soil represents those who hear the message and receive it with joy.

But like young plants in such soil, their roots don't go very deep. At first they get along fine, but they wilt as soon as they have problems or are persecuted because they believe the word. [These include those who are not seeking the Kingdom first in their lives, but this group has other problems also.]

The thorny ground represents those who hear and accept the Good News, but all too quickly the message is crowded out by the cares of this life and the lure of wealth, SO NO CROP IS PRODUCED. [These are more who are not seeking first the Kingdom, and this appears to be their primary issue.]

The good soil represents the hearts of those who truly accept God's message and produce a huge harvest—thirty, sixty, or even a hundred times as much as had been planted. [THESE ARE THOSE WHO ARE ON FIRE FOR GOD, ARE MAKING HIM SUPREME IN THEIR LIVES, AND ARE SEEKING FIRST HIS KINGDOM ABOVE EVERY OTHER THING IN THEIR LIVES.] (NLT)

Do any of you know someone who is truly on fire for God, and seems to stay that way? Can you picture someone in your mind whose actions, behavior, and words make it clear that they make Jesus their supremacy? They always have a good word, they are selfless in nature, and always seem to be giving instead of taking? They are always talking about God and His Word? Does it not make sense that God's blessings seem to be overflowing to people like this? I am not talking about fame and wealth (you don't have to have fame and wealth to be blessed by God), and I am not talking about a life without trials and tribulations (for the trials in life come to us all). But I am talking about having needs met, living in divine protection, experiencing abundant life, and having true joy about them, DESPITE THE TRIALS OF LIFE. I am talking about the ability to NAVI-GATE through the icebergs of life successfully.

You see, the only good and fertile ground is that of a person who has made God their supremacy, preeminence, and put Him in first place, above all others.

Colossians 1:18

He is the head of the body, which is the church. Everything comes from him. He is the first one who was raised from the dead. So IN ALL THINGS JESUS HAS FIRST PLACE. (NCV)

Jesus must have FIRST PLACE in our lives—above our jobs, our hobbies, and yes, even our families. Our Lord Himself told us in Luke 14:26

If you want to be my follower you must love me more than your own father and mother, wife and children, brothers and sisters—yes, more than your own life. Otherwise, you cannot be my disciple. (NLT)

We MUST seek first the Kingdom of God.

We MUST not try to fill voids with the things of this world. The void is there because God isn't!

We MUST not let the cares of this life and the lure of wealth choke out the Word of God. If we do, Jesus Himself said that no crop would be produced!! Jesus was not just kidding around! This was not written for everybody else but you! I am convinced that this is one of the most common roadblocks to receiving in the Church.

Jesus is telling us quite clearly that we will not produce a harvest unless the seed, the Word of God, falls on "fertile soil."

Jesus is clearly telling us that if the "message is crowded out by the cares of this life and the lure of wealth," no crop will be produced.

Jesus clearly tells us that we cannot serve two masters, or we will love one and hate the other.

Jesus clearly tells us that we cannot serve Him and money.

Jesus clearly tells us how all the "things" of life are added unto us, and that is by seeking FIRST His Kingdom and His righteousness.

This message cannot be any simpler, and it cannot be more clear and plain. Jesus Himself interpreted the parable of the Sower!! We do not have to rely on a Bible commentary to understand it!!! This point needs no colorful illustration, funny anecdote, or interesting side commentary for us to hear it, understand it, and remember it! It simply cannot be more clear.

Jesus is urgently and emphatically telling us:

SEEK ME FIRST!

MAKE ME FIRST PLACE!

SEEK MY KINGDOM!

SEEK MY RIGHTEOUSNESS!

DON'T SERVE MONEY OR WEALTH OR THE LURES OF THIS LIFE!

BUILD YOUR TREASURES UP IN HEAVEN!!!!

THEN, MY CHILD, THEN AND ONLY THEN, WILL YOU GET THE "THINGS"!

Seeking first the things, filling our spiritual void with things, and not making Jesus first place in our lives, is a roadblock to receiving the blessings provided for us by Christ Jesus.

HOW DO WE DEVELOP A DEEP AND LASTING RELATIONSHIP WITH GOD?

HOW DO WE SEEK FIRST THE KINGDOM OF GOD?

We develop a deep and lasting relationship with God the same way we would develop a deep and lasting relationship with anyone.

We spend time with that person.

We talk to that person.

We may even write that person a letter or send him or her a card.

We respect that person.

We listen to what that person has to say.

We are polite and thank that person if they do something for us.

We might even start to like that person so much that we start talking like that person.

We would probably go out of our way to do things that make that person happy.

We would say nice things to that person.

We would have a deep devotion for that person, wouldn't we?

It really is very simple to develop a deep and personal relationship with God, that will make Him first place in our lives, that will make Him a priority in our lives, that will allow us to seek first His Kingdom and not the "things." All we have to do is think what we would do in the natural and do those things.

NOW FOR ME PERSONALLY:

Praying is how I talk to God.

Reading His Word is how I listen to Him.

Praising Him is how I say nice things about Him.

Serving Him makes Him happy, so I serve Him because I love Him, not because I am trying to get something from Him.

I thank Him constantly for everything He has done for me, and I know what He has done for me because I listen to Him by reading His Word.

I talk like Him, because I admire Him and aspire to be like Him.

I am here to tell you that if you choose to run towards God, He is standing there with His arms open wide. The Bible says if we draw near to God, He will draw near to us. Some of us, if we would just turn around and look at Him, we would see Him, and He would catch up with us because He is constantly moving towards us because He loves us. Some of us, if we would merely stop running away from God, we would sense His presence coming up behind us.

Let's get to know God.

Let's talk and visit with God.

Let's listen to God by reading His Word.

Let's crave God.

Let's look forward to our times with God.

Let's treat Him like a best friend.

Let's start talking and acting like God, because we love Him and respect Him, not because we want something from Him. Let's seek ye first the Kingdom of God and His righteousness, and then let's let all the THINGS be added unto us.

CHAPTER 3

IN VAIN THEY WORSHIP ME

Matthew 15:9

And IN VAIN THEY WORSHIP ME, teaching as doctrines the commandments of men. (NKJV)

We as Christians simply do not have to accept (and indeed we have been commanded not to) the advice, the counsel, the teachings, the ideas, and standards of this world. We are not to be satisfied with any book, program, advice, or church that teaches us ideals or concepts that are not in line with the Word of God.

The Word of God is our standard.

The Word of God is the basis of our belief system.

The Word of God teaches our values.

The Word of God is our precept as Christians.

The Word of God tells us how we live and move and have our being.

Jesus had a word or two to say about those who teach man-made doctrine or doctrine that falls outside the Word of God. Jesus said they worship Him in vain, that their worship is a farce!! Jesus said that those who replace God's commands, who replace God's Word, with their own man-made teachings, are worshiping Him in vain!!!

Matthew 15:9

And IN VAIN THEY WORSHIP ME, teaching as doctrines the commandments of men. (NKJV)

This verse in the *New Living Translation* says,

THEIR WORSHIP IS A FARCE, for they replace God's commands with their own man-made teachings.

We as Christians are to live by God's teachings, God's commands, God's precepts, God's notions, God's way of doing things, NOT BY OUR OWN MAN-MADE TEACHINGS, NOTIONS, AND STANDARDS!!! If we live by our own teachings, our worship is a farce!!!

Jesus then told us how to handle those books, programs, TV shows, churches, teachers, co-workers, experts, etc. who proclaim these ideas and notions.

Matthew 15:14

SO IGNORE THEM. They are blind guides leading the blind, and if one blind person guides another, they will both fall into a ditch. (NLT)

Jesus even tells us in this same verse what will happen if we don't ignore them: We will fall into a spiritual ditch.

Matthew 15:14

Let them alone. They are blind leaders of the blind. And if the blind leads the blind, BOTH WILL FALL INTO A DITCH. (NKJV)

Now, do you think it might be a bit difficult to receive from God if you are lying in a spiritual ditch?

Someone may ask, "But will following worldly advice and counsel really hurt us?" Jesus said you will fall into a ditch, AND in the book of John, He said it will rob you of your belief in Him!!! We all know that our belief and faith in Christ Jesus are of paramount importance in receiving His blessings! YES!! Jesus is telling us it WILL hurt us if we follow worldly advice and counsel!!!!!

John 5:43-44
> *For I have come to you representing my Father, and you refuse to welcome me, even though you readily accept others who represent only themselves. No wonder you can't believe! For you gladly honor each other, but you don't care about the honor that comes from God alone. (NLT)*

Our beliefs and our faith are actually hindered by accepting others who represent or give worldly counsel and advice!!!

Someone might question, "So I am not to love the things of this world at all?" Well, first let's define "the world." Then we will see what God has to say about it.

The Greek word for "world" is *kosmos,* and *kosmos* means order and arrangement. So in the present world system, the ethically bad sense of the word refers to the order or arrangement under which Satan (whom the Bible calls the god of this world in 2 Corinthians 4:4) has organized the world of unbelieving mankind upon his principles of force, greed, selfishness, ambition, lust, and pleasure. This world system, this *"kosmos,"* is imposing and powerful with military might. It is often outwardly religious, scientific, cultured, and elegant, but it is dominated by satanic principles.

"The world" is the order and arrangement of unbelieving mankind and is based on force, greed, selfishness, ambition, lust, and pleasure.

The organization of force, greed, selfishness, ambition, lust, and pleasure. So any advice, book, counsel, idea, notion, standard, or concept that is CONTRARY to the Word of God HAS ITS ROOTS IN THE WORLD, IN *KOSMOS*, EVEN IF it appears harmless on the outside or at first glance. The Word of God is OUR STANDARD, as Christians, and it contains the order and arrangement of the Kingdom of God system, not the world system (the order and arrangement of unbelieving mankind). If an idea is not consistent with the Word of God, it is of the world, NO MATTER HOW HARMLESS it first appears. It indeed may be a "wolf in sheep's clothing," so to speak.

So after defining "the world," I ask again, is it okay to love the things of this world, things that are not consistent with the Word of God? Things that are intertwined with the order and arrangement of force, greed, selfishness, lust, ambition, and pleasure? What does God have to say about this matter?

1 John 2:15-16

LOVE NOT THE WORLD, NEITHER THE THINGS THAT ARE IN THE WORLD. If any man love the world, the love of the Father is not in him. For all that is in the world, the lust of the flesh, and the lust of the eyes, and the pride of life, is not of the Father, but is of the world.

That's pretty clear. It is hard to explain that one away, isn't it?

God clearly gives us the same message in the book of James.

James 4:4

Do you not know that FRIENDSHIP WITH THE WORLD IS ENMITY WITH GOD? Whoever therefore wants to be a FRIEND OF THE WORLD makes himself an ENEMY OF GOD. (NKJV)

We are given even more warnings about "wandering beyond" the teachings of Christ.

2 John 8-9

WATCH OUT, so that you do not lose the prize for which we have been working so hard. Be diligent so that you will receive your full reward. For if you WANDER BEYOND THE TEACHING OF CHRIST, you will NOT HAVE FELLOWSHIP WITH GOD. But if you continue in the teaching of Christ, you will have fellowship with both the Father and the Son. (NLT)

In these verses, God is telling us the same thing that Jesus told us. Accepting man-made doctrine is dangerous and puts us out of fellowship with God. In this same passage, God says that anyone who encourages a person who brings such teaching actually "becomes a partner in his evil work."

2 John 10-11

If someone comes to your meeting and does not teach the truth about Christ, don't invite him into your house or encourage him in any way. ANYONE WHO ENCOURAGES HIM becomes a PARTNER IN HIS EVIL WORK. (NLT)

So you see that the ideas, the standards, the notions, and the concepts of this world are not for us. If we are associated with any such notion or standard that is outside of the Word of God (I like to use the word "unscriptural"), then we are VULNERABLE to attack. We are giving the enemy a foothold or an opportunity. We must remain vigilant and challenge ANY teaching or concept that is contrary or outside the Word of God. Vulnerability to Satan can rob us of our rights and privileges and blessings in Christ.

According to Jesus Himself, accepting anything not consistent with or contrary to the Word of God can make us fall into a ditch and rob us of our beliefs and our faith! Accepting a worldly notion or standard can and will be a roadblock to receiving our blessings in Jesus Christ!!!

CHAPTER 4

REPENT AND DO THE FIRST WORKS

Jesus spoke these words to the church at Ephesus:

Revelation 2:4-5

Nevertheless I HAVE THIS AGAINST YOU, that you have left your first love. Remember therefore from where you have fallen; REPENT AND DO THE FIRST WORKS, or else I will come to you quickly and remove your lampstand from its place—unless you repent. (NKJV)

Contrary to what some believe, repentance is not merely saying you're sorry and asking for forgiveness. It is more than that! To repent is to feel such remorse, such regret for past conduct, so as to change yourself for the better. You feel bad for doing something or not doing something, to the point where you sincerely and genuinely desire to change!!!! The Hebrew word for "repent," as used in the Old Testament, actually means "to turn." You are moving in one direction, and you make a decision "to turn" and go in the other direction. The Greek word for "repent," as used in the New Testament, literally means "to think differently" as a result of deep remorse.

THAT attitude, the attitude of repentance, that attitude of, "Oh Lord God, I am so tired of living this way. I am so sorry that I have strayed down the wrong path. I am weary and broken, and I know that I have not been living according to Your will. I want You in my life, and I want to live for Jesus," is the softness of heart that allows the Holy Spirit to operate, to perform miracles, and to change lives. Teaching on repentance is NOT a message of condemnation. The concept of repentance deals with just the opposite: God's grace and mercy. In fact, the Word of God clearly teaches the forgiveness of sins upon confession of our sins.

1 John 1:9

If we confess our sins, He is faithful and just to forgive us our sins and to cleanse us from all unrighteousness. (NKJV)

God tells us that we are His righteousness through Jesus:

1 Corinthians 5:21

For He made Him who knew no sin to be sin for us, that we might become the righteousness of God in Him. (NKJV)

As His righteousness through Christ, God will not even remember our sins after they have been blotted out:

Isaiah 43:25

I, even I, am He who blots out your transgressions for My own sake; and I will not remember your sins. (NKJV)

The message of repentance is not making the claim that our lives should be without sin for us to inherit the blessings of God, for that would be inaccurate and unscriptural. The message of repentance after salvation underscores the importance of changing your desires and behavior once sin in your life is recognized and addressed.

So let's see what God has to say about this topic, and in particular how it relates as a roadblock to receiving His blessings. Remember, we are not talking about the presence of sin as a roadblock to receiving, rather the lack of repentance of the sin. There is a HUGE difference between the two. How can the lack of repentance keep you from receiving the blessings and gifts that are yours in Christ, as a child of God?

What does God have to say about the matter? According to the book of Acts in *The Amplified*, repentance is changing your mind and purpose once sin is recognized in your life. Repentance is the act or process of changing; the sincere desire TO CHANGE.

Acts 3:19

So repent (CHANGE YOUR MIND AND PURPOSE); turn around and return [to God], that your sins may be erased (blotted out, wiped clean), that times of refreshing (of recovering from the effects of heat, of reviving with fresh air) may come from the presence of the Lord. (AMP)

Notice, it says, "Turn around and return to God." I am NOT talking about backsliding—there could merely be AN AREA of our lives that we have recognized as sinful and have made ZERO attempt to change. ZERO!

What else does the Bible say about repentance? Repentance is one of the principles of the doctrine of Christ!

Hebrews 6:1

Therefore leaving the PRINCIPLES OF THE DOCTRINE OF CHRIST, let us go on unto perfection; not laying again the foundation of REPENTANCE FROM DEAD WORKS, and of faith toward God.

Repentance from dead works—changing your mind and purpose from sin—is one of the basic principles of the doctrine of Christ. In fact, the writer of Hebrews describes it as elementary, and as milk, not strong meat. The writer of Hebrews wanted to move on to other doctrines and topics, because repentance from dead works was already something the Church should know about and be practicing because it is so basic. Repentance from dead works is one of the basic principles of the doctrine of Christ!!! Can you see that the lack of such a principle in your life can be a roadblock to receiving?

What does God have to say about the importance and necessity of repentance? Jesus had something very important to say to the church at Ephesus about repentance.

Revelation 2:4-5

Nevertheless I have this against you (Jesus said to the church at Ephesus), that you have left your first love. Remember therefore from where you have fallen; repent and do the first works, or else I will come to you quickly and REMOVE YOUR LAMPSTAND FROM ITS PLACE—unless you repent. (NKJV)

Jesus told the church at Ephesus, comprised of saved, Spirit-filled believers, that if they do not repent, if they do not change their mind and purpose, back to the state they had been in (their first love), then He would remove their lampstand from them. He would take away the blessings, prosperity, and organization of their church, their assembly. Literally, He would "unchurch" them. Now, if Jesus can "unchurch" the Ephesians because they won't repent and do the first works, He can "unchurch" us.

JESUS IS SENDING A VERY CLEAR MESSAGE TO THE CHURCH HERE!!

Paul actually told the church in Corinth that he was HAPPY that they were sorry for their sins, and that their sorrow led to repentance, that their sorrow led to changing their ways and purpose. And then he told them WHY he was so happy that they repented.

2 Corinthians 7:9-10
> *NOW I REJOICE, not that you were made sorry, but THAT YOUR SORROW LED TO REPENTENCE. For you were made sorry in a godly manner, that you might suffer loss from us in nothing. For GODLY SORROW PRODUCES REPENTENCE LEADING TO SALVATION, not to be regretted; but the sorrow of the world produces death. (NKJV)*

God is telling us that being sorry that we have sinned, having godly sorrow, leads to repentance (changing your mind and purpose) and thus LEADS TO salvation—healing, deliverance, soundness, preservation, etc.

Okay then, what does sorrow WITHOUT repentance lead to? What does being sorry WITHOUT changing your mind and purpose lead to?

2 Corinthians 7:10
> *But SORROW WITHOUT REPENTANCE is the kind that RESULTS IN DEATH. (NLT)*

So just being sorry for your actions, without repenting, without a sincere desire to not make the same bad choice, without making an attempt to change your behavior, that kind of sorrow is NOT godly sorrow, and it results in death.

I am NOT talking about the presence of sin. Do not get me wrong. Don't misunderstand me. We are the righteousness of God through Christ, and if we confess our sins, God is faithful and just to forgive us our sins and to cleanse us from all unrighteousness, and He will remember our sins no more. The presence of sin is not the roadblock we are talking about here, but the LACK OF REPENTANCE for the sin.

Repentance is more than just SAYING you are sorry. That type of sorrow, the Bible says, leads to death. The type of godly sorrow that leads to salvation, that will keep us from Jesus removing our lampstand, that type of sorrow produces REPENTANCE, which is more than just words. Godly sorrow is accompanied by a sincere desire and effort to change behavior, thought processes, and purposes.

So you can begin to see that persisting in a certain behavior that you know is sin, without a sincere desire to change, can rob you of your rights and privileges, your blessings, in Christ. However, godly sorrow associated with repentance, associated with a sincere desire and effort to change, that kind of sorrow leads to salvation—healing, deliverance, soundness, wholeness, preservation, and safety.

So who are the people who are going to be filled with blessings?

Who are the people who are going to be filled with peace when the trials of life occur? Who are the people who will be filled with the healing power of Jesus Christ when sickness and disease sneak into their lives?

Who are the people who are going to be filled with all their needs being met?

Who are the people who will be filled with deliverance from bondages?

Who are the people who are going to be filled with the freedom from fear as they walk through the valley of the shadow of death?

Who will be filled?

In Matthew 5:6, Jesus says

> *Blessed are those who HUNGER AND THIRST FOR RIGHTEOUS-NESS, for they shall be filled.* (NKJV)

Those who actually crave God's righteousness, like a hungry man would crave a meal, or a thirsty man would crave a glass of cold water, those who will crave His righteousness will be filled. (Have you had such a hankering for some vittles that it just could not be suppressed?) That kind of hunger, that kind of craving, is what I am talking about here. Jesus said it will be those who have such a hankering for God's righteousness that they hunger for it, that they thirst for it, it is THOSE who will be filled. Can you see how godly sorrow that leads to repentance is associated with this craving for righteousness?

What are some other results, according to scripture, of an impenitent heart? What are some other results, according to scripture of sorrow without a desire in your heart to change? What does God have to say about that? In a letter to the church at Rome, an assembly of saved, Spirit-filled believers, God said:

Romans 2:5

But in accordance with your hardness and your IMPENITENT HEART you are TREASURING UP FOR YOURSELF WRATH in the day of wrath and revelation of the righteous judgment of God. (NKJV)

Do you think that treasuring up for yourself wrath might be a road-block to receiving the blessings of God? It doesn't take a mature Christian to understand that concept, does it? An impenitent heart is a heart that is comfortable enough with the presence of sin that no true desire to change is present. An impenitent heart will treasure up the wrath of God, and will certainly be a roadblock to receiving His blessings through Christ.

Paul told the church at Corinth that he would mourn or grieve for those who have not repented or changed their mind and purpose after they sinned.

2 Corinthians 12:21

Lest, when I come again, my God will humble me among you, and I SHALL MOURN for many who have sinned before and HAVE NOT

REPENTED of the uncleanness, fornication, and lewdness which they have practiced. (NKJV)

Why do you think Paul mourned for those lacking repentance in their lives? Because he knew that as a result they were living beneath their privileges as children of God. He mourned because he loved them as brothers and sisters in Christ, and it was sad to see them in such a state. He mourned because he knew that a heavy price was paid for their blessings, and they were keeping themselves from these blessings because of a lack of repentance.

Matthew 21:12-14

Then JESUS WENT INTO THE TEMPLE of God and DROVE OUT ALL THOSE WHO BOUGHT AND SOLD IN THE TEMPLE, and overturned the tables of the money changers and the seats of those who sold doves.

And He said to them, "It is written, 'My house shall be called a house of prayer,' but you have made it a 'den of thieves.'"

Then the BLIND AND THE LAME came to Him in the temple, and HE HEALED THEM. (NKJV)

Since the death, burial, and resurrection of Jesus, God's house is no longer the temple. His temple is our spirits. (1 Corinthians 3:16.) Jesus said, "It is written, 'My house shall be called a house of prayer,' but ye have made it a 'den of thieves.'"

After Jesus threw out the money changers and those who bought and sold from God's temple, what happened next? After Jesus cleansed God's holy temple, what happened next? After the temple of the Most High God was cleansed of commercialism and secularization, what happened next? The blind and the lame came to Him in the temple and He healed them. The blind and the lame came to Him in the temple and He healed them. The blind and the lame came to Him in the temple and He healed them.

THE BLIND AND THE LAME CAME TO HIM IN THE TEMPLE AND HE HEALED THEM!!!

Perhaps if the child of God were to purpose in his heart to rid his spirit, which is the very temple of the living God, of commercialism, secularization, the lure of wealth, and the cares of life, then and only then can the healing occur. How do we cleanse the temple of God? How do we cleanse our spirits of commercialism and secularization? We simply turn around. If we are walking in one direction and it is the wrong direction, we turn and walk the other way. We repent. Repentance cleanses the temple.

We most certainly can turn and walk the other direction, the path of wisdom, not the path of folly. We can do it because the Holy Spirit is our helper, and we can do all things through Christ who strengthens us. Repentance is possible for the believer, or God would not have told us to do it. If God instructed us to do something in His Word that was not possible, then that would be unjust, and God is not unjust. We CAN do it, we CAN repent, we CAN change our mind and purpose, simply because God says so. The Bible says it, I believe it, and that settles it for me.

Yes, we are the righteousness of God in Christ.

Yes, if we confess our sins, He is faithful and just to forgive us our sins and to cleanse us from all unrighteousness.

Yes, He has blotted out our sins, through Christ, and remembers our sins no more.

Yes, all that is scriptural truth and I praise God Almighty for His grace, for without it, we would have no hope.

But realize, that is only PART of the truth. PART of the truth can be a lie. PARTIAL truth can be TRUTH PERVERTED. Satan actually quoted scripture to Jesus in the wilderness when he was tempting Him.

Satan told Jesus a PARTIAL TRUTH when he told Him to throw Himself from the top of the temple because angels would catch Him lest He dash His feet against a stone. Jesus returned with the whole truth when He said, "It is written, thou shalt not tempt the Lord thy God." Partial truth can be perverted truth. The whole truth includes the doctrine of repentance.

Jesus Himself said in Luke 13:3

Unless you repent you will all likewise perish. (NKJV)

Godly sorrow that leads to repentance is scriptural; repentance from dead works is basic doctrine. The kind of sorrow for our sins that humbles us before God to the point that we crave His righteousness and desire to change our minds and our ways, THAT kind of sorrow and repentance is what leads to the blessings of God. As we can clearly see in studying the Word of God, lack of repentance in our lives can rob us of our rights and privileges in Christ.

CHAPTER 5

WALK NOT IN THE COUNSEL OF THE UNGODLY

Psalm 1:1

Blessed is the man that WALKETH NOT IN THE COUNSEL OF THE UNGODLY, nor standeth in the way of sinners, nor sitteth in the seat of the scornful.

There are very few topics that I have studied in the Bible that have more scripture regarding it than this one. As I was considering the importance of friends and acquaintances, I thought to myself, *I wonder what God has to say about it.* I mean, I have certainly heard sermons preached on it, and I have heard preachers comment on the subject and give their opinions on it. But I decided I wanted to know the real scoop firsthand from God Himself. After all, according to Jesus, a man's opinion, if not consistent with the Word of God, is nothing more than worldly doctrine and should be ignored, lest we fall into a ditch and it rob us of our beliefs in Jesus!

So, what does God have to say about who we should hang out with, who we should be friends with, and who we should associate with? How does God weigh in on this topic, and how can those WE CHOOSE to associate with actually be a roadblock to receiving our blessings in Christ?

Since the theme of what we are talking about is God's blessings in Christ, we will start with this scripture from Psalm 1:1 that discusses the company we keep AND talks about God's blessings.

> *BLESSED IS THE MAN that walketh not in the counsel of the ungodly, nor standeth in the way of sinners, nor sitteth in the seat of the scornful.*

This verse in *The Amplified* says,

> *BLESSED (HAPPY, fortunate, prosperous, and enviable) is the man who walks and lives not in the counsel of the ungodly [following their advice, their plans and purposes], nor stands [submissive and inactive] in the path where sinners walk, nor sits down [to relax and rest] where the scornful [and the mockers] gather.*

So we are blessed if we do not follow the advice of the ungodly; we are blessed if we do not stand submissive and inactive in the paths where sinners walk; we are blessed if we do not relax and rest where the scornful and the mockers gather.

What are we supposed to do then if we can't follow the advice of the ungodly, if we can't stand submissive in the path of a sinner, and if we can't hang out and rest where they gather? Let's look at verse 2.

> *But his DELIGHT IS IN THE LAW OF THE LORD; and in his law doth he meditate day and night.*

We delight in the law of the Lord, that's what we do!! We delight in His precepts, His teachings, His instructions, and we meditate on them habitually. Instead of hanging out with and following the advice of sinners, we are to delight ourselves in God's Word, and meditate on it as a consistent and habitual behavior!!

Then, how will we be blessed if we do that, instead of hanging out with and taking the advice of the ungodly? Let's look at verse 3.

And he shall be like a tree planted by the rivers of water, that bringeth forth his fruit in his season; his leaf also shall not wither; and WHATSOEVER HE DOETH SHALL PROSPER.

I don't know about you, but I want to be like a tree planted by the rivers of water. I don't know about anyone else, but I want to bring forth fruit. I don't know about the rest of the world, but I certainly do not want my leaf to wither, and I ABSOLUTELY want to prosper in what-soever I doeth!!!

So this is the first section of scripture that clearly tells us who NOT to hang out with, what we should be doing instead, and how we will be blessed if we follow these instructions.

Someone may say, "Well, okay, I can see that. I know I shouldn't participate when people around me do wrong things, but can keeping their company actually corrupt me? Can keeping the company of ungodly people, AS LONG AS I DON'T DO ANYTHING WRONG MYSELF, actually corrupt me? I mean, is sin really infectious?"

That is a good question, so I say we let God weigh in, seeing that it is a pretty important topic.

1 Corinthians 15:33

Do not be misled: "BAD COMPANY CORRUPTS GOOD CHARAC-TER." (NIV)

That is clear. There isn't much interpretation necessary with this verse. God says plainly and clearly that bad company corrupts good character. Let's see what else God has to say about it.

Galatians 5:9

But it takes only ONE WRONG PERSON among you to INFECT ALL THE OTHERS—a little yeast spreads quickly through the whole batch of dough! (NLT).

Now, we not only know that bad company corrupts good character, but God also says that one wrong person among us can INFECT US!! Infect us with what? He is talking about sin! Let's keep going.

1 Corinthians 5:6

How terrible that you should boast about your spirituality, and yet you let this sort of thing go on. Don't you realize that if EVEN ONE PERSON is allowed to go on sinning, soon ALL WILL BE AFFECTED? (NLT)

So according to God, bad company corrupts good character.

According to God, one wrong person among you can infect you with sin.

According to God, one person allowed to go on sinning will affect you all.

According to God, we are not to relax and rest where sinners gather.

According to God, we are not to take the counsel of the ungodly.

"Well, it sounds to me like you are telling us to act like 'holier-than-thou,' stuck- up Christians!" NOT AT ALL. NOTHING COULD BE FURTHER FROM THE TRUTH. Humility and meekness of spirit is a fruit of the Spirit and is important. SO IS LOVE. We as Christians are to love no matter what. We are to be nice to Christians and non-Christians alike. We are to help those in need. We are to give to the poor. We are to LOVE our enemies, as well as our friends. BUT SOMETIMES WE NEED TO LOVE SOME PEOPLE AT A DISTANCE AND WITH OUR PRAYERS—AND NOT LOVE THEM WITH OUR CLOSE PERSONAL FRIENDSHIPS.

Matthew 16:11-12

So again I say, "BEWARE OF THE YEAST of the Pharisees and Sadducees." Then at last they understood that he wasn't speaking about yeast or bread but about the FALSE TEACHING of the Pharisees and Sadducees. (NLT)

One of my favorite sections of scripture in Proverbs is in the first chapter. The Father is telling His child about three very important ideas involved with gaining wisdom. The Father describes three things that are important elements in the ability to navigate through life successfully.

Proverbs 1:7-10

FEAR OF THE LORD is the BEGINNING OF KNOWLEDGE. Only fools despise wisdom and discipline. LISTEN, my child, to what your FATHER TEACHES YOU. Don't neglect your MOTHER'S TEACHING. What you learn from them will crown you with grace and clothe you with honor.

My child, if SINNERS ENTICE YOU, TURN YOUR BACK ON THEM! (NLT)

This is one thing that I diligently teach my children. On the way to taking Drew to school, I leave the radio off so we can either talk or just have some moments of quiet without surrounding noise. I will ask Drew this question frequently: "What are the three things that are important for getting wisdom?" He will promptly answer, "Fear of the Lord, obey your parents, and stay away from bad people." It is just that automatic. I want that to be scriptural doctrine that is engrained in his head from a very young age.

"But what if when we are around them, we stay strong and resist the temptation. If we resist, we will be stronger, right? I mean, what if we resist? Will we STILL be led astray?" Good question. Let's ask God.

Proverbs 12:26

The godly give good advice to their friends; the wicked LEAD THEM ASTRAY. (NLT)

"Yeah, but will we really suffer harm just being around them? Is it really dangerous?"

Proverbs 13:20

Whoever walks with the wise will become wise; whoever walks with fools WILL SUFFER HARM. (NLT)

"Okay, but is it really DANGEROUS to hang out with them?" God, can You help us with this question?

Proverbs 22:24-25

Keep away from angry, short-tempered people, or you will learn to be like them and ENDANGER YOUR SOUL. (NLT)

So again I ask, is sin infectious?

Well, according to God, our character can be corrupted by bad company.

According to God, one wrong person among us can infect all the others.

According to God, if one person is allowed to go on sinning, soon all will be affected.

According to Jesus, false teaching is like yeast that can "leaven the whole lump."

According to God, we are to turn our back on sinners if they entice us.

According to God, the wicked will lead us astray.

According to God, if we walk with fools, we will suffer harm.

According to God, we endanger our soul if we associate with angry, short-tempered people.

According to God, we won't be blessed if we rest and relax with them in the places where they gather.

Someone else may say, "All that may be true, but I heard a preacher say once that we should spread our 'Jesus germs' on ungodly people, and not worry about them corrupting us!!" Children of God, how long are we going to use that as an excuse to hang around people we absolutely know we should not be hanging around?

"But I am going to witness to them about Jesus." Have you told them about Jesus? Have your witnessed the gospel of Christ to them? If you have, have they accepted or rejected it? Jesus had some very specific instructions for those who have rejected the message. How long are we going to use that as an excuse to hang around with and buddy up with those people whom we KNOW we shouldn't?

How many beers are you going to drink with these "friends" before you admit to yourself that you have made no effort whatsoever to tell them about Christ?

How many Internet chat rooms are you going to enter before you admit to yourself that bad company corrupts good character?

How many nights out are you going to engage in before you admit to yourself that you will suffer harm if you walk with fools?

How many bars are you going to frequent with these friends before you admit to yourself that you are endangering yourself?

How many ungodly movies are you going to see with them before you admit that you are being led astray?

How much gossip are you going to exchange with this person before you realize that you are infected?

How many ungodly sexual comments are you going to tolerate from this person until you start making those same comments yourself?

How many crude jokes are you going to listen to until you start saying them yourself?

Fear the Lord, listen to your parents (and for us adults, that means our Heavenly Father), and stay away from bad people. My ten and twelve year olds know it. We should too.

"Yes, but I may be the closest they ever come to Jesus." I have to tell you, that may indeed be true. You may very well be the closest that person gets to Jesus, and that is sad because getting close isn't quite good enough, is it? They need to give their heart to Jesus, and if they don't, if they just get close to giving their heart to Jesus, then that is just not good enough, is it?

Never stop loving them, mind you; never stop loving them, for we are commanded to love. We are NOT to be "holier-than-thou," stuck-up Christians. But you may have to stop loving them with your personal friendship and your personal time and start loving them with your prayers. Sometimes it is easier to love someone with your prayers than it is with your personal friendship.

"Yes, but Jesus hung out with harlots and tax collectors and sinners!!" No, He didn't. I said, "No, He didn't." Jesus WITNESSED to sinners many times at the invitation to a wedding, a dinner, or a social event, but Jesus was the guest of honor. Those attending were interested in His gospel, and many repented and began to follow Jesus. Luke 15:1 NKJV tells us that the tax collectors and sinners "drew near to Him to hear Him." Jesus witnessed to sinners who drew near to Him to hear Him.

Jesus spent time with sinners who were repentant and wanted to hear His Word. For those who did not want to hear His Word, He told them not to cast their pearls before swine. (See Matthew 7:6.) And at the end of a hard day of preaching the gospel to sinners, to whom did Jesus return? With whom did He relax, rest, recline, and enjoy fellowship? His disciples and followers, that's who. Jesus reached out to those who were accepting of His message. He DID NOT hang around ungodly people for social reasons and participate in their sinful activities. But He kept loving them, didn't He? He loved them so much He gave His very life for them, even though they were sinners.

"Yes, but the Bible tells us to go into all the world, telling people the good news about Jesus. How can I tell people about Jesus if I don't associate with them?"

True, we must reach out to the ungodly and to sinners. However, we are not to participate in their sinful acts in the process. I will say that again: We have been commissioned to tell the ungodly about Jesus. However, we are not to participate in their sinful acts in the process. And according to scripture, associating with ungodly people in a social manner can infect us and corrupt us.

"Okay, so then who are we supposed to hang out with?" God has a bit of advice on that too.

2 Timothy 2:22

Run from anything that stimulates youthful lust. Follow anything that makes you want to do right. Pursue faith and love and peace, and ENJOY THE COMPANIONSHIP OF THOSE WHO CALL ON THE LORD WITH PURE HEARTS. (NLT)

So God tells us to enjoy the companionship of those who call on the Lord with pure hearts, those who pursue faith, love, and peace. That is clear. Let's see what else the Word has to say:

2 Corinthians 6:14-18

DON'T TEAM UP WITH those who are UNBELIEVERS. How can GOODNESS be a partner with WICKEDNESS? How can LIGHT live with DARKNESS? What harmony can there be between CHRIST and the DEVIL? How can a BELIEVER be a partner with an UNBELIEVER? And what union can there be between GOD'S TEMPLE and IDOLS? For we are the temple of the living God.

As God said: "I will live in them and walk among them. I will be their God, and they will be my people. Therefore, come out from them and SEPARATE YOURSELVES from them, says the Lord. DON'T TOUCH their filthy things, and I will welcome you. And I will be your Father, and you will be my sons and daughters, says the Lord Almighty." (NLT)

So our companions, our friends, and the people we associate with socially and team up with should be Christians. They should be believers. This scripture is not telling us to completely segregate ourselves from nonbelievers. No, not at all. We are to go into all the world telling people about Jesus. It is merely saying to separate ourselves, as God has separated us, or sanctified us through Christ. Love them, yes. Tell them about Jesus, yes. Help them, yes. But don't team up with them, and don't partner up with them.

What are some other qualities of a godly friend?

Proverbs 27:17

As iron sharpens iron, so a man SHARPENS THE COUNTENANCE of his friend. (NKJV)

A godly friend will sharpen your countenance. Merely hanging around a godly friend will improve you. A godly friend will also love at all times. A godly friend's motivation will be love, not self.

Proverbs 17:17

> *A friend LOVES at ALL TIMES…. (NKJV)*

The Bible also tells us to follow the steps of good men, not sinners!

Proverbs 2:20

> *FOLLOW THE STEPS OF GOOD MEN instead, and stay on the paths of the righteous. (NLT)*

So hang around and associate with someone who will sharpen your countenance.

Find a friend who builds you up in your faith.

Hang around those godly men and those virtuous women.

Hang around someone who will sharpen your countenance.

Someone who will improve you.

Someone you can learn from.

Someone who displays godly wisdom.

Someone who loves at all times.

Someone who is good.

Someone who is righteous.

And finally, a question that is well-deserved: Where can I find a friend like that? If it weren't for my non-Christian friends with bad habits and behaviors, I wouldn't have any friends at all. Where am I going to find a friend who sharpens my countenance, someone who improves me, someone I can learn from, someone who displays godly wisdom, someone who loves at all times, and who is good and righteous?

The answer is two-fold. First, you begin to be that person. You begin to display the character of a godly friend. (If you build it, they will come.) Second, pray for this friend. Create a scriptural prayer based on the Word of God asking God to put someone like that in your life.

In the meantime, examine your friendships, and understand the scriptural importance of hanging with the right crowd, and its effect on receiving the blessings of God.

CHAPTER 6

SPIRITUAL GROWTH: WE SHOULD NO LONGER BE CHILDREN

Ephesians 4:14-15

That WE SHOULD NO LONGER BE CHILDREN, tossed to and fro and carried about with every wind of doctrine, by the trickery of men, in the cunning craftiness of deceitful plotting, but, speaking the truth in love, may GROW UP IN ALL THINGS INTO HIM who is the head—Christ. (NKJV)

We probably all know and understand that God expects us to grow spiritually, to grow and mature in our spiritual walk. But can lack of spiritual growth actually be a hindrance to receiving our blessings in Christ? Instead of trying to figure it out on our own, or listen to someone's opinion on the matter, or pontificate back and forth between each other until we come up with a concept that sounds good to us, instead of all that, let's see what God has to say about the topic.

A quick review on what scripture says about growing up and maturing in our Christian walk starts in Ephesians 4:14-15 which is given above. But let's look at it again:

> *That we SHOULD NO LONGER BE CHILDREN, tossed to and fro and carried about with every wind of doctrine, by the trickery of men, in the cunning craftiness of deceitful plotting, but, speaking the truth in love, may GROW UP IN ALL THINGS INTO HIM who is the head— Christ. (NKJV)*

So God wants us to move past childhood spiritually and grow up in all things into Christ. Why? So we won't be "tossed to and fro" with false doctrine, with advice, ideas, or notions that are contrary to the Word of God. God wants us to mature spiritually so that we are not deceived by man-made doctrine (those who teach as doctrine the commandments of men). God wants us to experience spiritual growth so we will SPEAK THE TRUTH IN LOVE.

Just in this one section of scripture we learn some of God's thoughts on growing up spiritually:

1. He wants us to move past spiritual childhood.

2. Spiritual childhood is characterized by vulnerability: false doctrine, the trickery of men, the cunning craftiness of men, and the deceitful plotting of men.

3. Spiritual growth is characterized by speaking the truth in love.

That's a lot of information in just two verses of scripture! Let's keep going!

I Peter 2:1-2

> *Therefore, laying aside all malice, all deceit, hypocrisy, envy, and all evil speaking, as newborn babes, desire the pure milk of the word, THAT YOU MAY GROW THEREBY. (NKJV)*

Here God tells us that He wants us to grow spiritually, which is accompanied by laying aside malice, deceit, hypocrisy, envy, and all evil speaking. God is associating spiritual growth with the laying aside of all these undesirable characteristics!!

"Yeah, but does it REALLY matter if I mature spiritually or not? What happens if I just stay right where I am—not backslide or anything—just not move forward spiritually?"

The writer of Hebrews is actually scolding church members in this next passage:

Hebrews 5:12-14

In fact, though by this time you ought to be teachers, you need someone to teach you the elementary truths of God's word all over again. You need milk, not solid food! Anyone who lives on milk, being still an infant, is NOT ACQUAINTED WITH THE TEACHING ABOUT RIGHTEOUSNESS. But solid food is for the mature, who by constant use have trained themselves to DISTINGUISH GOOD FROM EVIL. (NIV)

According to God, it most certainly matters!! In fact, God says only with spiritual growth, with moving forward in our spiritual walk with an ever ceaseless craving to know God better, can we learn to distinguish good from evil!! And without spiritual growth, without getting to know our Lord Jesus better, we are not acquainted with the teaching about righteousness!!

Can you think back when you first became a Christian, when you were a spiritual babe? At that point in your spiritual walk, you actually were not acquainted with the teaching of righteousness. In essence, you did not know good from evil in many instances! Why? Because you were a spiritual babe, that's why! Just as you did not know right from wrong when you were a toddler, you relied on the teaching and direction from your parents to keep you safe. You didn't know that a stove was hot. You didn't know to look both ways before you crossed a street. You didn't know not to talk to strangers. You didn't even know how to tie your shoes or dress yourself until your mother or father showed you how!!! This very same immaturity is present spiritually when you first become a Christian, and you needed to take instruction from your Father through His Word to be able to distinguish good from evil.

I heard a minister on TV say that when he first became a Christian, he did not know what fornication was. He actually did not know that God did not want us to have sexual relations with anyone that is not our married spouse!! He told how he read about fornication while reading the Bible one day, and he had to look up the definition of the word in the dictionary. When he found out what it meant, it was like, "Oh my goodness! I did not know that was wrong. I never knew. I will have to stop!"

Spiritual maturity is necessary to distinguish good from evil! What else does God have to say about growing spiritually?

Philippians 1:9-10
> *This is my prayer for you: that YOUR LOVE WILL GROW MORE AND MORE; that you will have knowledge and understanding with your love; that you will see the difference between good and bad and will choose the good; that you will be pure and without wrong for the coming of Christ. (NCV)*

Here again is a scriptural prayer for spiritual growth in love, the consequences of the spiritual growth being knowledge, understanding, discerning good and bad, and purity.

Okay, so God expects us to grow spiritually so we won't be vulnerable to false doctrine or to the deceit and cunning craftiness and trickery of men. He expects us to mature spiritually so we speak the truth in love, and lay aside malice and deceit and hypocrisy and envy. So God wants us to grow so we can tell the difference between good and evil and make right choices. I buy into all that, but we are talking about roadblocks to receiving the blessings of God in Christ, and I want to know what God has to say about that! I mean, if I stop growing spiritually, does God say that it actually HINDERS my blessings? If I just stay where I am spiritually, without moving forward OR backward, can my blessings be hindered?

2 Peter 1:5-9

> *Do your best to improve your faith. You can do this by adding goodness, understanding, self-control, patience, devotion to God, concern for others, and love. IF YOU KEEP GROWING IN THIS WAY, it will show that what you know about our Lord Jesus Christ has made your lives useful and meaningful. BUT IF YOU DON'T GROW, you are like someone who is NEARSIGHTED or BLIND, and you have forgotten that your past sins are forgiven. (CEV)*

God says "If you don't grow, you are like someone spiritually nearsighted or blind!" If you don't grow, you will forget the basics and not ever know or realize that you have lost anything! He didn't say as long as you don't backslide, or as long as you just stay the same. He said:

IF YOU DON'T GROW,

IF YOU DON'T IMPROVE YOUR FAITH,

IF YOU DON'T INCREASE YOUR GOODNESS,

IF YOU DON'T GROW IN YOUR UNDERSTANDING,

IF YOU DON'T MATURE IN YOUR SELF-CONTROL,

IF YOU DON'T BEAR MORE FRUIT OF PATIENCE, YOUR DEVOTION TO GOD DOES NOT GROW,

IF YOU DON'T INCREASE IN YOUR CONCERN FOR OTHERS, YOUR LOVE…

IF ALL THESE THINGS DON'T GROW AND MATURE AND BECOME MORE COMPLETE…then you are like someone who is nearsighted or even blind to the point that you have forgotten that your past sins are forgiven.

I ask you, can anyone who is spiritually nearsighted or blind to the point they have forgotten that Jesus died for the forgiveness of their sins ever expect to receive any of the blessings of God in Christ? Of course they can't! And this is the problem with many Christians who have remained spiritually deplete and failed to grow. They get to the point where they don't even know that they are not living a spiritual life, and they are wandering around and stumbling around in darkness, and not in the light!!! They can't get the devil out of their physical bodies in the form of sickness and disease, because they are hanging on to the devil in some other aspect of their life, and they are so spiritually blind and nearsighted because they have failed to grow that they don't even know it!!! I am not talking about backslidden Christians and neither is the Bible. God is talking about the FAILURE TO ADVANCE IN YOUR SPIRITUAL WALK. God is talking about Christians who are LUKE-WARM and who are merely standing still spiritually. God is talking about Spirit-filled, church-going, tithing believers WHO ARE SIMPLY NOT GROWING SPIRITUALLY.

Very clearly, God is saying that when we fail to grow spiritually, we become nearsighted and blind spiritually. In the Kingdom of God system, there is only ONE WAY, and that is forward. NO STANDING STILL IS ALLOWED. If we stand still, we can't see; we can't discern; we stumble and don't know why; we are in the dark. We can't even see where we are going. The darkness has blinded us.

Look what God says about walking and living in the dark:

1 John 2:11

But he who hates (detests, despises) his brother [in Christ] is in dark-ness and walking (living) in the dark; HE IS STRAYING and does NOT

PERCEIVE OR KNOW where he is going, because the darkness has blinded his eyes. (AMP)

"So are you telling me that because I have merely relaxed spiritually; because I have not made a constant effort in my life to establish a more intimate relationship with God; because I have taken a spiritual vacation; because I stopped seeking God through constant, daily, habitual reading of His Word; because my prayer life is basically non-existent; because I spend more time on the Internet or watching TV than I do with God; because I have started to view church as something I HAVE to go to and not something I CRAVE—just because of all that, I am HINDERING MYSELF from receiving my blood-bought blessings in Christ? Is that what you are telling me?"

No, I am not telling you that at all. God is!

Jesus said this to the assembly of Spirit-filled believers in Laodicea:

Revelation 3:15-16

"I know your works, that you are neither cold nor hot. I could wish you were cold or hot. So then, BECAUSE YOU ARE LUKEWARM, and neither cold nor hot, I will VOMIT YOU OUT OF MY MOUTH." (NKJV)

Now I don't know what being "vomited out of God's mouth" means. I JUST KNOW THAT IT'S BAD AND I DON'T WANT IT!! I will let the theologians sit back and debate and interpret that statement. I simply know that I want no part of it!

Someone may say, "That sounds like a warning to me! What are you trying to do, anyway, WARN ME? It sounds like you are trying to warn me with shame!!!"

To this accusation, I can only go the Word of God and respond. God said in 1 Corinthians 4:14:

ROADBLOCKS TO RECEIVING

I do NOT WRITE THESE THINGS to SHAME YOU, but as my beloved children, I WARN YOU. (NKJV)

God tells us to grow spiritually in His Word, not to ruin our fun and make us miserable. He, as our Creator, knows how to make us happy and knows what will create lasting joy in our lives. One of those things is spiritual growth. He tells us to grow spiritually because He LOVES US. He warns us what will happen if we don't grow spiritually because HE LOVES US. Just as a parent would warn his child on the dangers of talking to strangers or just as a mother would warn her child on the dangers of smoking, our Heavenly Father most certainly is warning us of the danger of not growing spiritually. A scriptural warning should NEVER be interpreted as discrediting, shaming, or condemning, but rather as a message of LOVE from our Heavenly Father who cares for us and loves us.

So in summary, according to God, we should no longer be children.

According to God, we should grow up in all things into Christ.

According to God, spiritual children are tossed to and fro and vulnerable to false doctrine.

According to God, spiritual childhood is accompanied by vulnerability to the trickery of men, to the cunning craftiness of deceitful plotting.

According to God, spiritual maturity is associated with "speaking the truth in love."

According to God, growing spiritually is coupled with the laying aside of malice, deceit, hypocrisy, envy, and evil speaking.

According to God, those who have failed to advance themselves spiritually are "not acquainted with the teaching about righteousness."

According to God, only the spiritually mature can train themselves to distinguish good from evil.

According to God, your spiritual growth in love will be connected to knowledge and understanding.

According to God, spiritual stagnation will cause spiritual nearsightedness or spiritual blindness. You will wander around in spiritual darkness and not even perceive where you are going.

According to Jesus, staying spiritually lukewarm positions you to be vomited out of God's mouth.

I don't know about anyone else, but...

I don't want to be a spiritual child anymore.

I want to grow in Christ.

I want to speak the truth in love.

I don't want to be vulnerable to false doctrine and find myself in a spiritual ditch.

I don't want to be vulnerable to the trickery, cunning craftiness, and deceitfulness of men.

I want to speak the truth in love and not be tossed about to and fro with every wind of doctrine.

I don't know about anybody else, but...

I want to advance my spiritual walk.

I want to read my Bible!!

I want to lay aside malice, deceit, hypocrisy, envy, and evil speaking.

I want to be acquainted with the teaching about righteousness.

I don't know about anybody else, but...

I want to read my Bible!!

I want my love to grow and abound so I will know the difference between right and wrong and choose right.

I want to strengthen my relationship with Jesus!!

I want to be connected to knowledge and understanding!!

I want to successfully navigate through the icebergs of life!!!

I don't know about anyone else, but I like to see where I am going!!! Hallelujah!! (I MUCH prefer the high beams on my car, because I can see so much more.)

I do not want to wander around in darkness, stumbling over every little thing.

I want to see where I am going!!

I want to walk AROUND the stumbling blocks and not trip over them because I am spiritually nearsighted!!!

I WANT TO READ MY BIBLE!!

I don't know about anybody else, but I want to position myself to receive the blood-bought blessings of God.

I do NOT want to lollygag around in a lukewarm "every day's a struggle" type atmosphere.

I don't want to be vomited out of the mouth of God!! NO!!

I don't know about anybody else, but I want to approach my Father through His Word. I want to turn off my TV, put a hold on my projects and toys, put down my *Cosmo* and *People* magazines and open God's Word. It may just come to that...actually having to seek God through His Word when I am at home, and not just limiting God to the three or four hours a week I spend at church. It may just come to that!

SPIRITUAL GROWTH: WE SHOULD NO LONGER BE CHILDREN

If we fail to grow spiritually, if we fail to mature as Christians, if we fail to advance in our Christian walk and our relationship with God, we are in the dark. We become so spiritually blind or nearsighted that we don't know the difference between right and wrong. We become so spiritually blind that we even forget about what Jesus did on the cross. It actually gets to the point where God wants to vomit us out of His mouth. We take ourselves completely out of position to receive His blessings, and all this is from mere LACK OF GROWTH. This is all from merely staying lukewarm. Staying stagnant spiritually.

These scriptures tell us this is what happens when we FAIL TO CONTINUALLY MATURE AS CHRISTIANS. This very well may be a HUGE reason for the failure to receive God's blessings in Christ. Is the lack of spiritual growth robbing you of your rights and privileges in Christ?

CHAPTER 7

EFFECTIVE PRAYER: MAY THE WORD ABIDE IN YOU

John 15:7-8

> *If you abide in Me, and MY WORDS ABIDE IN YOU, you will ask what you desire, and it shall be done for you. By this My Father is glorified, that you bear much fruit; so you will be My disciples. (NKJV)*

Prayer is more than just shouting words out into the atmosphere. The Word of God has many things to say about praying to God, and I think God wants us to know about prayer, and I think He expects us to know what His Word says about prayer. This is not meant to be an exhaustive study on prayer; however, if we are to receive the blessings of God, we need to know HOW to pray, WHAT to pray for, and what NOT to pray for.

If our prayers are not being answered, we need to ask ourselves what is wrong on the sending end, not on the receiving end. God never changes, and He loves to answer prayer and shower us with blessings. So if our prayer life is ineffective, we need to examine our prayer life and see how it can grow and be improved.

Jesus had much to say about prayer. For instance, He put some conditions on answered prayer.

John 16:23-24

And in that day you will ask Me nothing. Most assuredly, I say to you, WHATEVER YOU ASK THE FATHER IN MY NAME He will give you. Until now you have asked nothing in My name. Ask, and you will receive, that your joy may be full. (NKJV)

God is our Father, and we can approach Him in the name of Jesus. When we approach our Father according to His Word, He is sure to hear us. We are to pray to God the Father in the name of Jesus. We are not to pray to Mary, Peter, or any other saint. Jesus told us we are to pray to the Father in the name of Jesus.

Look what else Jesus had to say about answered prayer:

John 15:7-8

IF YOU ABIDE IN ME [The Amplified says, "Abide vitally united to Me"], and MY WORDS ABIDE IN YOU, you will ask what you desire, and it shall be done for you. By this My Father is glorified, that you bear much fruit; so you will be My disciples. (NKJV)

A real prayer life must be based on the Word of God. The condition set by Jesus Himself is that His Word abides in you, and then you shall ask what you will and it shall be done unto you. Jesus Himself let us know under the New Covenant that this important condition be present for us to receive answers to our prayers.

What does it mean to "abide in Jesus"? Let's ask God.

1 John 2:6

He who says he ABIDES IN HIM ought himself also to WALK JUST AS HE WALKED. (NKJV)

We are to "abide in Christ." We are to strive to walk as He walked. We are to learn about Him, know His Words, and familiarize ourselves with the way He responded to certain situations. We are to live our lives as He did, and to do this we must know Him better.

These two conditions on answered prayer that Jesus set forth by His words are amazingly important, and tie together with many of the other roadblocks we have identified. Here, however, they specifically relate to ANSWERED PRAYER.

A real, scriptural, working prayer life must be based on God's Word.

God never changes. He is in the business of answering prayers. All through the Bible He says to call on His name, and He will answer us. But we must remember the conditions given by Jesus under the New Covenant. When you know God's Word, you know what to ask for. When you are familiar with God's Word, you can pray in faith. Otherwise, you are praying in the dark. If you are praying in the dark, then you are praying out of faith. We need to learn to pray in the light.

How do we go about praying in the light? What does God have to say about praying in the light? What can we do that gives us light?

Psalm 119:130

The ENTRANCE OF THY WORDS giveth light; it giveth understanding unto the simple.

The entrance of thy words giveth light.

When God's Word enters, light is there. Light is accompanied by God's Word. A little Word...a little light. A lot of Word...a lot of light. But the entrance of His Word gives the light. God is saying that light is given when His words are taught, understood, are meditated on. Without His Word, there is darkness. If God's Word ABIDES in you, Jesus said then you will ask what you desire, and it will be done for you. "If ye abide in me, and my words abide in you"…you are enlightened, in effect, is what the Word tells us.

If you don't know what the Word says about the particular subject you are praying for, then you are not enlightened. If you're not enlightened, then you are not in the light on that particular subject. You may be on other subjects, but on that particular subject you are not in the light if you don't know what God's Word has to say about it.

If you're not in the light you are in the dark. Praying in the dark is prayer based on unbelief and doubt. You pray not really knowing if it is God's will, or not really knowing if you should be asking for that particular thing, or praying not really knowing if God is listening.

Praying in the light, on the other hand, is prayer based on faith. Praying in the light is knowing what God says in His Word, and believing that He is true to His Word. Praying in the light is praying in confidence. Praying in the light is knowing God's will on a certain matter, because you know what He says about it in His Word.

Some people are about halfway in between the light and the dark on some things. So many times His Word is not abiding in us, and so our praying is all wrong or out of kilter.

The more you know about the Word, the more fruitful prayer life you will have. The more Word that abides in you, the more effective prayer life you will have. The less you know about the Word, the less fruitful and the less effective your prayer life will be. "If ye abide in me, and my words abide in you," says Jesus. "If my words abide in you," Jesus said, "THEN your prayers will be answered."

EFFECTIVE PRAYER: MAY THE WORD ABIDE IN YOU

When people come to me and ask that I pray for them, or pray with them, I ask, "What scripture are you standing on?" because I know the condition set by Jesus on the subject of prayer. If they say that they are not really standing on any scripture, then they are praying in the dark and out of faith. But if I can help them see what God's Word says about that particular subject, then they are enlightened because the entrance of His Word giveth light. Now that we are enlightened and out of the dark, out of doubt and unbelief, out of not knowing whether it is God's will for them or not, we can agree together in faith and see results.

I have said it many times and I will say it many more. Find scriptures that pertain to the things you are praying for. Then you have a solid foundation for faith and for your prayer life.

What does the Word of God say? What does God have to say about it? We need to get so Word-conscious that no matter what happens, no matter what the situation we come across, no matter what crisis occurs in life, we will ask ourselves, "What does God have to say?" We need to base our belief system on the Word of God.

God said He will honor His Word. He said He will watch over HIS WORD to perform it. He said HIS WORD will not return to HIM void.

Jeremiah 1:12

Then said the LORD unto me, Thou hast well seen: for I will hasten (The Amplified says, "Watch over") my word to perform it…

Isaiah 55:11

So shall My word be that goes forth from My mouth; It SHALL NOT RETURN TO ME VOID, but it SHALL ACCOMPLISH what I please, and it SHALL PROSPER in the thing for which I sent it. (NKJV)

Some people say, "Yeah, but I don't understand His Word." He didn't say to understand it. He said to believe it. As a matter of fact, He said to lean not on our own understanding.

Proverbs 3:5

> *Trust in the LORD with all your heart, and LEAN NOT ON YOUR OWN UNDERSTANDING. (NKJV)*

I don't understand it either sometimes, I just believe it.

Others will say, "Well, it is obvious that I have this or that this is a problem. Why should I have to ask God for it? God knows I need it and if He loves me, He will provide it. Why do I have to read the Bible just to know how to ask Him for something?"

Good question. What does God have to say about that? After all, Jesus said, "For your Father knows the things you have need of BEFORE YOU ASK Him" (Matthew 6:8 NKJV). So it is true that our Father knows what we need before we ask, but He still wants us to ask.

Matthew 7:7-8

> *ASK, and it will be given to you; seek, and you will find; knock, and it will be opened to you. For everyone who asks receives, and he who seeks finds, and to him who knocks it will be opened. (NKJV)*

So God still wants us to ask Him and to seek Him, EVEN IF He already knows what we need. The problem is not that God knows or doesn't know what we need.

The issue is that WE OFTEN DON'T KNOW WHAT WE WANT OR NEED OURSELVES. WE THINK WE KNOW WHAT WILL MAKE US HAPPY, BUT WE DON'T REALLY KNOW UNLESS HIS WORD ABIDES IN US!!!!

God requires that His Word abide in us, because if it does not, we will not know what things to ask for that are actually good for us. Remember, in John 16:24 NKJV He said, "Ask, and you will receive, that your joy may be full." If we ask for something not in line with His Word, which is His Will, then God, as our Father and Creator, knows that it will not make our joy full. He, as our Father and Creator, our God, knows what is good for us and what is not. If we are not familiar with His Word, then we won't know what is good for us and what is not!!!! We won't know what God has to say on the matter. We will be merely asking based on our own human, fleshly desires!!

For instance, if we ask for $10 million, it would probably not make our joy full. We probably could not handle it if His Word was not abiding in us. It would probably lead to a very destructive period in our lives if His Word was not abiding in us, like most, if not all, lottery winners. Or if we ask for a new friend, but we don't know what the Word has to say about what kind of friends we should have (and thus we do not have His Word abiding in us), then gaining a friend without the characteristics that God says a friend should have, would not bless us. It would not make our joy full. I could go on and on, but the point is that God knows how our joy is to be full, and that requires that His Word abide in us.

John 15:7

If ye abide in me, and my words abide in you, ye shall ask what ye will, and it shall be done unto you.

God wants to hear and answer your prayers. If He didn't want to, He would not have told you how to get the answers!!! Because He loves you, because He is your Father, He had the Holy Spirit to inspire men to write His words while He was on the earth. So you see, a real prayer life is based on the Word of God. Whether or not you will get answers depends on KNOWING GOD'S WORD.

I am so glad that I learned this a few years ago. I mean, I got into the Word with everything that I had, because I realized through my inward witness that having God's Word abide in me was the answer to everything. It was the answer to my prayer life, it was the answer to problems in my family, it was the answer to my financial issues, it was the answer to my business problems, and it was the answer to my health and my restoration to what had been stolen from me.

I just got into the Word, and put everything else out. Now, that is when you are going to get real results with God, whether it is healing, deliverance, peace, or finances. Jesus said, "If my words abide in you." You will have to get into the Word for His words to abide in you. IT MAY EVEN COME TO THE POINT THAT YOU MAY HAVE TO READ THE BIBLE AT NIGHT INSTEAD OF WATCH A MOVIE!

Find out what God has to say about whatever it is that you are praying about, organize and focus your prayer based on these scriptures, and deliver your prayer in faith. I mean, what else can you do? You prayed God's Word directly back to Him, and now you let God do His part. Stay out of fear, doubt, and unbelief, and stand on your scriptures in faith!! Make a decision to believe God, to believe what God says in His Word, despite contradictory circumstances in the natural. The more Word, the more faith. Faith comes by hearing the Word of God. (Romans 10:17.) The more faith, the more answered prayer.

You see, if there seems to be no other hope, sometimes that is the only thing that makes us turn to God and His Word. When medical science has failed, when every relationship seems to end up the same way, when you can no longer control what your child is doing, when your spouse betrays you and you have nowhere else to turn, when you don't see any possible way out, you absolutely must rely on God. Sadly enough, this is what it takes to motivate some people to really dig into

His Word, seek a relationship with Him through His Word, and learn about how to get answers to prayer through His Word.

What does the Word say?

John 15:7

If ye abide in me, and my words abide in you, ye shall ask what ye will, and it shall be done unto you.

Are your prayers being answered? If the answer is no, it is probably because God's Word is not abiding in you to the extent that it should. This roadblock of an ineffective prayer life is overcome by God's Word abiding in you.

CHAPTER 8

LOVE YOUR NEIGHBOR AS YOURSELF

In answering a question by a Pharisee lawyer, Jesus replied,

Matthew 22:37-40

> *"Love the Lord your God with all your heart and with all your soul and with all your mind." This is the first and greatest commandment. And the second is like it: "Love your neighbor as yourself." All the Law and the Prophets hang on these two commandments. (NIV)*

Jesus Christ, our Lord and Savior, the Son of Almighty God, the very person whom we have invited into our hearts and the very person whom we have confessed as our Lord, He is the One who gave us only two commandments. He told us that the first and greatest commandment is to love the Lord our God with all our heart, all our soul, and all our mind. And the second, which is like unto it, to love our neighbor as ourself.

Someone may say, "Why only two commandments? I thought there were ten commandments? Why are there only two commandments now?"

That is a good question, and Paul's letter to the Christian assembly in Rome helps us out with this:

Romans 13:9

For the commandments, "You shall not commit adultery," "You shall not murder," "You shall not steal," "You shall not bear false witness," "You shall not covet," and if there is any other commandment, are all SUMMED UP in this saying, namely, "You shall love your neighbor as yourself." (NKJV)

So under the New Covenant, or the New Testament, God tells us that any and all previous commandments are SUMMED UP in the great commandment of love—you shall love your neighbor as yourself. And, of course, Jesus said, "All the other commandments and all the demands of the prophets are BASED ON THESE TWO commandments" (Matthew 22:40 NLT).

Just in case you haven't bought into the idea that the Ten Commandments have been replaced, or summed up in Jesus' two commandments of love, let's look at Galatians 5:14:

The ENTIRE LAW IS SUMMED UP in a single command: "Love your neighbor as yourself." (NIV)

If you think about it, if you show someone love and love them as you love yourself, you will not steal from them, you will not lie to them, you will not sleep with their spouse, you will not kill them, etc.

"Okay, so what does all this have to do with roadblocks to receiving? Why is walking in love so important?"

First of all, we should probably take note of this "love concept" if Jesus told us that all the previous commandments, all the previous law and scripture of the prophets, are summed up in this one concept.

Then it is probably pretty important, and we should learn as much about it as possible.

Secondly, God tells us that love is accompanied by manifestations and blessings. The Bible teaches that love is accompanied by manifestations and blessings. Jesus had this to say about it:

John 14:21

He who has My commandments and keeps them, it is he who loves Me. And he who loves Me will be loved by My Father, and I WILL LOVE HIM AND MANIFEST MYSELF TO HIM. (*NKJV*)

So Jesus said that love is accompanied by manifestations. All of a sudden our eyebrows lift with interest and curiosity! I mean, it is the manifestations that we are learning about here, and we are trying to find out what God has to say about why they are not showing up in our lives.

If we are seeking the blessings of God...

If we want God's promises to manifest in our lives...

If we are standing in faith and believing God for answered prayer...

If we are looking to RECEIVE from God by faith...

If we are wondering why things are not showing up in our lives, even though we sincerely believe God's Word...

Then it would probably do ourselves some good to show Jesus that we truly love Him, and we are not just trying to get something from Him.

It would probably do us good to show Jesus that we are sincere about our love for Him. And according to Jesus Himself, "He who has My commandments AND KEEPS THEM, it is he who loves Me."

As uncomfortable as this message may be, I cannot merely skip over it quickly. If we believe the Bible, then we must understand that Jesus told us here, and in numerous other places, that if we truly love Him, then we will keep His commandments. We indeed confessed Jesus as our Lord, but have we truly given Him lordship? Or did we give Him lordship at one time, and then slowly took it back. Jesus said, "If you love Me, you will keep My commandments."

Is God the Father like a vending machine to us, just Someone we come to when we need something from Him? Or do we truly love Him with all our hearts, souls, and minds? Do we truly love God? Jesus said, "If you love Me, if you truly love Me (not just lip service, but sincere love), you will keep My commandments, and I only gave you two." LOVE IS ACCOMPANIED BY MANIFESTATIONS AND BLESSINGS!

The Holy Spirit inspired the apostle Peter to tell us that if we love our enemies, instead of repaying them with evil or insult, then we will "inherit a blessing."

1 Peter 3:9-10

Do not repay evil with evil or insult with insult, but with blessing, because to this you were called SO THAT YOU MAY INHERIT A BLESS-ING. For, "Whoever would love life and see good days must keep his tongue from evil and his lips from deceitful speech." (NIV)

What kind of blessing are we going to inherit if we show love? Peter said we would love life and see good days!!!!! Hallelujah!!! That pretty much covers it! Glory to God!!! I mean, is there really anything more that we could ask for or want or need other than loving life and seeing good days? These are the two ultimate blessings!!! God says we will love life and see good days if we show love!!!

Are days that you are sick and in the hospital good days? Certainly not!

Are days spent in poverty good days? Absolutely not!

Are days spent arguing with your spouse good days? I don't think so!!

Are days worrying about your children who have strayed away good days? Of course not!!!

Are days spent in fear, doubt, and unbelief good days? Certainly not!!

Are days spent in turmoil good days? Absolutely not!!

Are days spent in the depths of a bondage good days? No!!!

God is telling us to LOVE instead of repaying evil with evil!

God is telling us to LOVE instead of repaying insult with insult!

God is telling us to LOVE instead of speaking evil!!

God is telling us to LOVE instead of speaking deceit!!!

And what will be the result? WE WILL INHERIT A BLESSING!!! WE WILL INHERIT THE BLESSINGS OF LOVING LIFE AND SEEING GOOD DAYS!

LOVE IS ACCOMPANIED BY MANIFESTATIONS AND BLESSINGS!

"Okay, I am starting to see the importance of walking in love…so what is love anyway? I mean, as long as I am here, I might as well find out more about this love issue. It seems to be pretty important, and I must admit that loving life and seeing good days sounds pretty good. So what is love anyway?"

God told us exactly what love is in 1 Corinthians 13, and I like *The Amplified Version:*

1 Corinthians 13:4-8

Love endures long and is PATIENT and KIND; love NEVER IS ENVIOUS nor boils over with jealousy, is NOT BOASTFUL or vainglorious, does not display itself haughtily.

It is NOT CONCEITED (arrogant and inflated with pride); it is NOT RUDE (unmannerly) and does NOT ACT UNBECOMINGLY. Love (God's love in us) does NOT INSIST on its own rights or its own way, for it is NOT SELF-SEEKING; it is NOT TOUCHY OR FRETFUL OR RESENTFUL; it takes no account of the evil done to it [it pays no attention to a suffered wrong].

It does not rejoice at injustice and unrighteousness, but rejoices when right and truth prevail.

LOVE BEARS UP under anything and everything that comes, is ever ready to believe the best of every person, its HOPES ARE FADELESS under all circumstances, and it ENDURES EVERYTHING [without weakening].

LOVE NEVER FAILS [never fades out or becomes obsolete or comes to an end].

Now I am not going into a detailed discussion about each of these characteristics of love, but I will tell you this: Personally, when I first began to recognize the importance of walking in love...

When I first became convicted to the truth that if I truly love Jesus, then I will obey His commandments of love...

When I first made the commitment to base my belief system on the Word of God...

When I first made the commitment to base my words and actions on the Word of God...

When I first realized that to live a truly Christian life meant to walk in love...

I knew I had to absorb this Word into my spirit, and I knew I had to do it on a continual basis. I wrote down these elements of love *from The Amplified* on index cards and read them and meditated on them over and over and over again. And slowly but surely I (and others around me for that matter) began to notice a change in my behavior and reactions toward others. It took time, it took discipline, it took effort; and there were no magic incantations or prayers that could replace my continual feeding on the Word of God to produce this fruit in my life. I still have to do this, and I will continue to feed on these scriptures if I want to maintain and improve my love walk!!

This Word of God MUST get into your spirit somehow for this fruit to show up in your life. And it won't get there unless you feed on it and read it and meditate on it HABITUALLY.

Generally, when we talk about love, we at some point enter into the topic of forgiveness. "So how does forgiveness tie into all this? Do you have to forgive someone in order to love them?" Good question. Let's see what God has to say about it:

Ephesians 4:31-32

Let all bitterness, wrath, anger, clamor, and evil speaking be put away from you, with all malice. And be kind to one another, tender-hearted, FORGIVING ONE ANOTHER, even as God in Christ forgave you. (NKJV)

Sounds like forgiveness is a pretty important aspect of love, or at least it is according to God...but let's keep going.

Colossians 3:12-14

Therefore, as God's chosen people, holy and dearly loved, clothe yourselves with compassion, kindness, humility, gentleness and patience. Bear with each other and FORGIVE whatever grievances you may have against one another. FORGIVE as the Lord FORGAVE you. And over ALL THESE VIRTUES put on LOVE, which BINDS THEM ALL TOGETHER in perfect unity. (NIV)

God says that LOVE binds all these virtues (compassion, kindness, humility, gentleness, and patience), including forgiveness, together!!!

One reason God ties in forgiveness with love is because LACK OF FORGIVENESS, LIKE LACK OF LOVE, CAN HINDER YOUR PRAYER LIFE AND FAITH.

"Come on now. How can lack of forgiveness hinder our prayer life?"

Jesus weighs in on this topic as He is teaching His disciples about prayer in the book of Mark.

Mark 11:25-26

And whenever you stand PRAYING (so the topic of this scripture is prayer), if you have anything against anyone, FORGIVE him, that your Father in heaven may also FORGIVE you your trespasses. But IF YOU DO NOT FORGIVE, neither will your Father in heaven FORGIVE your trespasses. (NKJV)

Jesus was talking about ANSWERED PRAYER in this scripture. He tells us not to even finish praying if there is unforgiveness in our lives. He then tells us that forgiveness is so important that God requires it…to the point that God will not forgive us our trespasses if we harbor unforgiveness AGAINST ANYONE!

Jesus also had this to say about forgiveness in the Sermon on the Mount.

Matthew 6:14-15

For IF YOU FORGIVE men their trespasses, your heavenly Father will also forgive you. But IF YOU DO NOT FORGIVE men their trespasses, neither will your Father forgive your trespasses. (NKJV)

"All right, all right, if Jesus said it, then it must be so. Jesus said I have to forgive or God won't forgive me. Okay, I buy it, but how does love affect our faith? I mean, I can believe for something in faith, and still not be ready to forgive my enemies, right?"

Interesting question. Not really a good question…but an interesting question. Let's see what God has to say.

Galatians 5:6

> *For in Christ Jesus neither circumcision nor uncircumcision avails anything, but FAITH WORKING THROUGH LOVE. (NKJV)*

I like the *New Living Translation* where it says, "For when we place our faith in Christ Jesus, it makes no difference to God whether we are circumcised or not circumcised. What is important is FAITH EXPRESSING ITSELF IN LOVE." *The Amplified Version* says, "Faith [is] activated and energized…through love."

According to God, our very faith expresses itself through love.

According to God, our faith works through love.

According to God, our faith is activated by love.

According to God, our faith is energized by love.

Jesus commanded us to forgive before we even finish praying!

According to Jesus, God won't even forgive our sins if we don't forgive those who sin against us!!!

So according to scripture our faith won't even work without love! If our faith won't work, then our prayers won't work. If we are without forgiveness, we are without faith. And the Bible tells us that it is impossible to please God without faith. Can you see how the love walk may just be an important issue when it comes to receiving the blood-bought blessings of God? Can you see that not walking in love can be a HUGE roadblock to receiving?

As our interest on the topic of love continues to rise, someone may ask, "Does God say anything about how He will treat us if we do not forgive?"

Jesus did in the Parable of the Unforgiving Debtor: Without going through the entire parable, let's look at the conclusion our Lord gave at the end of the parable.

Matthew 18:34-35

In anger his master turned him over to the jailers TO BE TORTURED, until he should pay back all he owed. This is how my heavenly Father WILL TREAT EACH OF YOU UNLESS YOU FORGIVE your brother from your heart. (NIV)

I encourage you to read the entire parable, but the conclusion drives the point home: Forgive your brother from your heart, or God will treat you like a tortured criminal!!

Someone in righteous indignation may say, "After all this scripture on love, it almost seems that if we are not walking in love, we don't even know God!!! I mean, yeah, I still haven't forgiven my friend for spreading that gossip about me, but I do know my God! I mean, yeah, I still haven't forgiven my boss for not giving me the promotion or the raise, but I still know my God! I mean, yeah, I certainly haven't forgiven the drunk driver who crashed into my car, but I still know my God! You are making it sound like if we don't walk in love, we don't even know God!!!"

First John 4:8 says,

He who does not love DOES NOT KNOW GOD, for God is love. (NKJV)

Then 1 John 4:20-21 says:

If someone says, "I love God," and hates his brother, he is a liar; for he who does not love his brother whom he has seen, how can he love God whom he has not seen? And this COMMANDMENT we have from

Him: THAT HE WHO LOVES GOD MUST LOVE HIS BROTHER ALSO. (NKJV)

The scripture is clear. There is more scripture pertaining to love than any other topic that I am aware of. It simply and clearly is a prerequisite for receiving from God. In fact, love MUST be our motivation. If we are motivated by anything other than love, the Bible tells us we are of no value whatsoever.

1 Corinthians 13:1-3
> *If I could speak in any language in heaven or on earth but didn't love others, I would only be making meaningless noise like a loud gong or a clanging cymbal. If I had the gift of prophecy, and if I knew all the mysteries of the future and knew everything about everything, but didn't love others, what good would I be? And if I had the gift of faith so that I could speak to a mountain and make it move, without love I would be no good to anybody. If I gave everything I have to the poor and even sacrificed my body, I could boast about it; BUT IF I DIDN'T LOVE OTHERS, I WOULD BE OF NO VALUE WHATSOEVER. (NLT)*

Other versions say that without love, I PROFIT NOTHING or I GAIN NOTHING. First Corinthians 13:3 NIV says, "But have not love, I gain nothing."

Are there areas in your life that you are waiting for God to show up, and it appears that you are gaining nothing?

Do you have a physical illness that you are believing God to heal, and you seem to be gaining nothing?

Are you praying for your children, and you seem to be gaining nothing?

Are you believing for financial increase, but you seem to be gaining nothing?

Are you standing in faith, and hanging tough in your marriage, but you seem to be gaining nothing?

Are you reading your Bible to seek peace, but you seem to be gaining nothing?

Are you standing strong in your deliverance from a bondage, but you seem to be gaining nothing?

Are you believing God for the manifestation of a promise you KNOW is in His Word, but you seem to be gaining nothing?

Are you faithfully tithing, and yet you seem to gain nothing?

The Bible says we can have it all: knowledge, the gift of prophecy, giving to the poor, speaking in the tongues of angels. The Bible says we can even have mountain- moving faith.Yet if we have not love, we gain nothing. If love is not our motivation, we gain nothing. We produce no crop. The seed is falling on thorny ground. If we don't love others, we are of no value whatsoever. If love is not our motivation, we gain nothing.

If our expectations in life are motivated by our desire for wealth and not love, we are of no value whatsoever.

If our demands of our spouse and children are motivated by selfishness, and not of love, we gain nothing.

If we continually and habitually insist on our own rights and our own ways, we will profit nothing.

If we are not kind and patient towards our spouse, and do not walk in love, we gain nothing and we forfeit our blessings.

If the Bible studies we lead are motivated by our quest for recognition, and not of love, we profit nothing.

If the dinner we cook at night is motivated by anything other than love, we are of no value whatsoever.

If the advancement of our career is motivated by greed, and not love, we gain nothing.

If our relationships are motivated out of lust, and not love, we are of no value whatsoever.

If our volunteer work in the church is motivated by pride and recognition, and not of love, we gain nothing.

If we keep account of the evil done towards us, we are of no value whatsoever.

If our tithes and offerings are motivated by ANYTHING other than love, they are of no value whatsoever.

If the day-to-day decisions in life are motivated by selfish desires, and not love, we gain nothing.

If our life visions and goals are motivated by the lure of happiness and wealth, and not of love, we gain nothing

"Well, for goodness sakes, you make it sound like if we don't have love, we may as well be dead!! I mean, there has to be more to this life than love!! Love cannot be the meaning of life, can it?"

First John 3:14 says,

> *If we love our Christian brothers and sisters, it proves that we have passed from death to eternal life. But a person who HAS NO LOVE IS STILL DEAD. (NLT)*

Now, this is talking about spiritual death, not physical death, but I ask you, "Which is worse?" Spiritual death, a life apart from God, is far worse than physical death in my book. I would MUCH RATHER be together with God in Heaven, than apart from God and alive on this earth. To me, spiritual death, being separated from God, is MUCH worse than physical death.

Is walking in love important?

Is the love walk necessary for receiving the blessings of God?

Can I live a Christian life without love?

Do I really HAVE to forgive? What if I don't?

Can the lack of love and forgiveness be a roadblock to receiving my blessings from God in Christ?

Can lack of love hinder my deliverance?

Can lack of forgiveness keep me from being healed?

Can not walking in love keep me in fear and out of peace?

If I choose to remain in unforgiveness, what will happen?

What about divine protection and financial blessings? Are they affected?

Can not walking in love really hinder my faith?

Can unforgiveness hinder my prayers?

Can returning evil for evil and railing for railing affect my blessings?

How can I find a life that I love?

How can I see good days?

Is the lack of love in my life really a roadblock to receiving?

Well, according to God, all the other commandments and all the demands of the prophets are based on the principle of love.

According to God, the entire law is summed up in a single command: "Love your neighbor as yourself."

According to Jesus, he who keeps My commandments, it is he who loves Me.

According to Jesus, He will manifest Himself to those who walk in love.

According to God, we will inherit a blessing if we choose to LOVE instead of speaking evil.

According to God, we will have long life and see good days if we LOVE instead of speaking insults and deceit.

According to God, we are to be kind to one another, tenderhearted, forgiving one another, even as God in Christ forgave us.

According to God, love binds all these virtues together (compassion, kindness, humility, gentleness, patience, and forgiveness).

According to Jesus, we are to forgive others before we even finish our prayers to God.

According to Jesus, if we don't forgive others, God won't forgive us.

According to God, our very faith actually works through love.

According to God, our very faith expresses itself in love.

According to God, our very faith is energized and activated by love.

According to Jesus, the Father will treat us with anger unless we forgive our brothers from our hearts.

According to God, if we don't walk in love, we don't even know God, for God is love.

According to God, he who loves God MUST love his brother also.

According to God, all knowledge, all wisdom, and all faith do us no good at all in the absence of love.

According to God, without love and forgiveness, we are facing a MAJOR ROADBLOCK to receiving.

CHAPTER 9

GET OUT OF
THE PAST

Philippians 3:13-14

> *Brethren, I do not count myself to have apprehended; but one thing I do, FORGETTING THOSE THINGS WHICH ARE BEHIND and reaching forward to those things which are ahead, I press toward the goal for the prize of the upward call of God in Christ Jesus. (NKJV)*

Can staying in your past hurt you? If we are unable to let go of the past and move on, will that actually hinder our blessings from God? Can our inability to shake off the past with all its pain actually rob us of our rights and privileges in Christ? Can self-pity poison our faith life? Many of us are aware that it would be to our benefit if we could get over a traumatic experience in our past, but what if we have been unable and incapable of letting go? Will we actually suffer harm? What does God have to say about it?

The scriptures are very clear on this subject, and there is much written. Living in the past IS toxic. It absolutely is a roadblock to receiving, and a hindrance to abundant life. If satan can get you to stay in your past, he can effectively produce a roadblock in your life to receiving the blessings of God through Christ.

Thinking about the past is dangerous ground. The past is a feeding ground for the enemy. We as Christians must not and cannot give the devil a foothold or an opportunity to instill the spirit of fear upon us by getting us to focus in on our past. If you find yourself meditating on your past mistakes, failures, and traumatic events, then you will likely find yourself vulnerable to the spirit of the devil, which is fear. As you keep your sights on where you are going instead of where you have been, there is less foothold or opportunity for the devil to place thoughts of fear and doubt in your mind. The devil wants you in your past, no matter how good things may be in the present.

Even though you have been delivered, the devil is still going to talk to you about where you have been and your past bondages.

Even though you have been healed, the enemy is going to try and make you focus on your past symptoms.

Even though your marriage has been restored, satan is going to try and make you think about all the past problems and betrayals.

Even though you are now saved and part of the Body of Christ and the righteousness of God, the enemy is going to make you try and remember all the bad things you have done.

Even though your finances are moving in the right direction, the devil will try and make you hesitant and fearful based on some of the failures of the past.

Even though you are beginning to experience good and perfect well-being, he will try and make you remember and rehash your past turmoil.

Even though you are beginning to be strong in the Lord and in the power of His might, the enemy will try and make you remember your failures when you tried to fight the battles on your own.

The apostle Paul certainly knew something about this subject, and the Holy Spirit inspired him to write:

Philippians 3:13-14

No, dear brothers and sisters, I am still not all I should be, but I am FOCUSING ALL MY ENERGIES ON THIS ONE THING: Forgetting the past and looking forward to what lies ahead, I strain to reach the end of the race and receive the prize for which God, through Christ Jesus, is calling us up to heaven. (NLT)

Paul is saying that he may not be all he should be, he may not be where he wants to be, he may not have captured and made his own everything that he should, he may not have become perfect yet, but he is focusing all his energies on THIS ONE THING!! And what is that? *Forgetting the past and looking forward to what lies ahead.* Here the Word of God is telling us to focus our energies on getting out of our past and look forward to what lies ahead. Why? So we can reach the end of the race and RECEIVE.

God is saying that if we stay in our past, and refuse to move forward to what He has planned for us, then we won't reach the end of the race and RECEIVE. Staying in our past is a ROADBLOCK TO RECEIVING!!!

THE THINGS WHICH ARE BEHIND WILL TRY TO KEEP YOU BEHIND!!!!! There must be a constant reaching forth to the things which are ahead of you.

Now listen to me carefully. Faith is based on the now, and fear is based on the past!!! The devil lives in the past, and he tells you what you used to do. Have you ever thought about the fact that the enemy is always talking about the past? God is always in the now. Faith is now, and if we are living life defeated, maybe we are living in the past. I don't know about you, but I do not want to be stuck in the past. There is too much waiting on me in my future. It's time to MOVE ON AND RECEIVE!!!

Jesus put it this way:

Luke 9:62

No one, having put his hand to the plow, and LOOKING BACK, is fit for the kingdom of God. (NKJV)

What Jesus is saying here is that you are ready to put your hand to the plow, you are ready to follow Him, you are ready to make Him first place in your life, you are ready to seek first the Kingdom of God, you are ready to grow spiritually, you are ready to walk in love, you are ready to walk by faith and not by sight. Then, all of a sudden you begin to look back, you begin to ponder, you begin to doubt, you begin to fear. Thoughts of the past create a fear of the future, and you look back. You had your hand to the plow ready to go, and then you looked back. What does Jesus say is the result of that?

Jesus says you are not fit for the Kingdom of God. He didn't say you were not fit for Heaven. He said you were not fit for God's way of doing things. In other words, you won't operate the way God requires you to operate in the Kingdom. And if you are not operating the way God requires, then it will be VERY difficult to remain in faith, receive your blessings by faith, and be a conqueror and consistently win battles.

God's requirement in the Kingdom is that you don't look back. His requirement for the Kingdom is that you don't stay in the past. And when a man puts his hand to the plow, and he takes his hands off and looks back, he is not fit for Kingdom operation, because you cannot operate in the Kingdom while you are stuck in the past. You can't do it. If you are going to operate in the Kingdom, you have to LET THE PAST GO!!! There are so many dear children of God suffering right now because they are stuck in the past and still holding on to something.

People who are still offended with something that happened in the past.

People who are hanging on to unforgiveness over something that happened in the past.

People who are not walking in love because of something that happened in the past.

People who are feeling guilty because of something that happened in the past.

People living in condemnation because of something in the past.

People living in self-pity because of the past.

People remaining in depression and emotional turmoil because of something in the past.

People hanging on to their bondages because of the past.

That's where all of satan and the kingdom of darkness is—IN THE PAST.

I CAN'T DOUBT IF I DON'T CONSIDER THE PAST. How am I going to doubt about the future if there was nothing in the past that gave me a reason to doubt? I CAN'T WALK IN UNFORGIVENESS IF I DON'T CONSIDER THE PAST, because unforgiveness deals with something in the past. I can't be prejudiced if I don't consider the past, because every spirit of division is based on something that has happened in the past. I can't be envious or jealous if I don't consider the past. I can't have a fear of the future without having a fear of the past. You know what that fear of the past does? It tries to stop you from accomplishing anything in the future.

Some of us are afraid of a bill because we couldn't pay one in the past.

Others are afraid of a disease or a virus because of what they have seen that disease or virus do to someone in the past.

Some Christians are afraid to tell someone about Jesus because they have been made fun of in the past.

Still others are afraid to ride in an airplane because of something that almost happened in the past.

Many are afraid to have healthy relationships because of the bad ones they had in the past.

Many more are afraid to trust anybody, because their trust was damaged in the past.

What else does God have to say about this topic?

Isaiah 43:18-19

FORGET THE FORMER THINGS; do not dwell on the past. See, I am doing a NEW THING! Now it springs up; do you not perceive it? I am making a way in the desert and streams in the wasteland. (NIV)

This is one of my favorite passages of scripture, and I prefer the *King James Versioni* because it is so poetically beautiful to me.

REMEMBER YE NOT THE FORMER THINGS, neither consider the things of old. Behold, I will do a NEW THING; now it shall spring forth; shall ye not know it? I will even make a way in the wilderness, and rivers in the desert.

God is asking us to not remember the former things. Then He tells us not to even consider the things of old. Don't even consider the things of old. Why? God is into NEW THINGS. I said God is into new things!!!! Quit trying to string out the old stuff as long as you possibly can. God wants to do some new things in your life. Okay, thank God for the old stuff, thank God for what He has already done. Thank God for where you have been, thank God for where He brought you out of, but God is getting ready to do something new, something you have never been in before, something you have never done before, because God is into NEW THINGS.

We can't do a new thing while we are still on the ground suffering from something that happened two, three, five, or ten years ago!!! We HAVE to get up and discover the NEW THINGS that God has for us! We must get up off the ground and RECEIVE His blessings through Christ Jesus. We must OVERCOME the roadblock of our past, and walk in the blessings of God.

Some people say, "Oh, have I messed up. I am in darkness. I have fallen." I love what God says through the prophet Micah. Micah is talking to his enemies.

Micah 7:8

Rejoice not against me, O mine enemy: WHEN I FALL, I SHALL ARISE; when I sit in darkness, the LORD shall be a light unto me.

What God is saying is that sometimes in our lives we fall; sometimes in our lives we find ourselves in darkness. But in that midnight hour of our life, we still wait on God. We wait on the Lord who is our Light, our Salvation, and we trust in God and KNOW that He will never leave us or forsake us. So we say to our enemies, we say to debt, we say to our problem, we say to our mountain, our storm, we say to our job, we say to our health, we say to our relationships, we say, "WHEN I FALL, I SHALL ARISE!!!!!!"

We make up our minds that we are living for the new things God has for us in our future, and we are not stuck in the past with all the old problems. We make up our minds that when we fall, we shall arise!!!! When we sit in darkness, our God is going to bring us into the light!!! We may have no idea what to do, but we know our God will let us know what to do. He will be working on it while we sleep, while we eat, while we go to school, while we love our children, while we go to church, and while we continue on with our life. God will be working and solving every problem that faces us !!!!

Genesis 41:50-52 says,

> *And to Joseph were born two sons…. Joseph called the name of the firstborn MANASSEH: "For God has made me FORGET ALL MY TOIL and all my father's house." And the name of the second he called EPHRAIM: "For God has caused me to be FRUITFUL in the land of my affliction." (NKJV)*

Joseph had two sons. The firstborn was named Manasseh, which means in Hebrew "causing to forget." The Bible tells us in verse 51 that he was named Manasseh "for God has made me forget all my toil and all my father's house." This was Joseph's FIRSTBORN.

Now if you remember, Joseph had a pretty awful past. He was sold into slavery by his very own brothers, then put in prison in Egypt because of a false accusation by Potiphar's wife. He had a lot to be bitter about, probably more reason to be bitter and angry and resentful than anyone we know. Joseph, however, did not wallow in self-pity DESPITE the awful circumstances in his life. No, Joseph remembered not the former things, neither did he consider the things of old. Why? Because he knew God had a NEW THING in store for him.

So Joseph, in the process of forgetting those things which were behind, and in the process of reaching forward to those things which were ahead, named his firstborn son Manasseh, for God had made him to forget all his toil.

Now, Joseph had a SECOND son. He named his second son Ephraim, which means in Hebrew "double fruit." The Bible tells us in verse 52 that he was named Ephraim "for God has caused me to be fruitful in the land of my affliction." This was Joseph's SECOND son. You see, Joseph's "double fruit" came AFTER his "causing to forget." For Joseph to be "fruitful in the land of his affliction," he first had to "forget all his toil." The message here is that your "double fruit" will come ONLY AFTER you "forget your toil."

The Lord may be speaking to you right now, saying, "If you are ever going to be fruitful, you will have to forget the toils, the offenses, the mistakes, and all the things that you have gone through in your past." Before there could be an Ephraim, there had to be a Manasseh. And before there is going to be a fruitfulness in your life, there is going to have to be a forgetting of those things that are in the past. I am telling you, if you hold on to those things of the past, then they will block up the fruitfulness that God wants you to have in your future.

Your fruitfulness includes the rights and privileges that belong to you as a child of God. Can you see that a lack of Manasseh in your life can be a roadblock to your Ephraim? The Manasseh must come before the Ephraim. The forgetting must come before the fruit. The past is a roadblock to your future.

This is why people who have been through terrible traumas in their life must choose to get out of their past. They must choose to get away from it because God is waiting in their future to restore them from everything that was stolen from them. But satan doesn't want them to forget, and if he can keep them in their past, and if he can keep them mad at the person who abused them, if he can keep them mad at the situation because it simply was not fair that they caught that disease, if he can keep them mad at that parent, the spouse, or the friend who mistreated them, if he can keep them using these past resentments as crutches in their life, then he can keep them from their fruit, their rights and privileges in Christ Jesus, their Ephraim.

You will never have your Ephraim until you let go of the stuff that happened in the past. You have to have Manasseh (remember, "Manasseh" means forgetting the toils of the past) before you can have Ephraim. Your fruitfulness; your blessings, are right in front of you, waiting on you to take those crutches and throw them away, and say, "You know what? Yes, I went through that and it hurt bad. Yes, I went through that and it was painful and it almost destroyed me, it almost killed me, but I PRESS ON FOR THE PRIZE...there is fruit waiting on me, and I am not going to let it spoil while I am sitting back in the past."

How many more counseling sessions are you going to have?

How many more shoulders are you going to cry on?

How many more friends are you going to have to recruit to "tell your story"?

How many more people, TV shows, books, or "experts" are you going to get bad advice from?

How many years down the road are you still going to be asking your church to pray for you because of that one terrible event that happened so many years ago?

How many more times are you going to actively refuse to forgive yourself because you have become so comfortable in self-pity?

If you tell your story, it should be in victory when you tell it. If you tell your story and ask for prayer, it should be in faith that my God will never leave you or forsake you. It ought not be with you still suffering from something that happened ten, twenty, thirty, forty, fifty, or sixty years ago, because there is an Ephraim waiting on you! There is an Ephraim waiting to be born in your life!! A time of fruitfulness. A time of receiving what Christ bought for you with His body and His blood. Hallelujah!

Let's make it happen, let's move on, and get on to where the victory is. It takes hard work to get over some things, but it is something that you absolutely must do to take your role as a conqueror in life through Him who loves you. How can you be a conqueror if the past still plagues you? How can you consistently win battles when thoughts of fear and panic based on past experiences dominate your mind and your heart? It just can't be done. There has to be a Manasseh before the Ephraim. You CAN control what you think about, and the more you practice on it, the better you will get!!! You CAN make a conscious decision to open the Bible and read instead of drown yourself in sorrows, self-pity, drugs, alcohol, etc., because self-pity will continue to keep you out of your Ephraim.

Living in your past is a MAJOR roadblock to receiving the blessings of God. If we put our hand to the plow and look back, we are not fit for the Kingdom of God according to Jesus. According to God, we need to focus all our energies on the prize that is ahead of us. According to God, we are not to remember the former things. According to God, we are not to even consider the things of old. According to God, He has for us a NEW THING, A FRUITFULNESS. According to God, our Manasseh must come before our Ephraim.

CHAPTER 10

WORRY AND FEAR: DESTROYERS OF FAITH

Matthew 6:25

> *Therefore I say to you, DO NOT WORRY about your life, what you will eat or what you will drink; nor about your body, what you will put on. Is not life more than food and the body more than clothing? (NKJV)*

Worry and fear are just as destructive and as bondage-producing as other habits, struggles, and hardships. Living in a state of worry and fear can keep you from receiving the blessings of God through Christ. Fear and worry are roadblocks to receiving.

The Bible, and indeed Jesus Himself, tells us not to worry. Worry is simply a milder form of fear. It is less intense, but more nagging than fear. It is less powerful, but more persistent than fear.

Jesus weighs in on the subject, because He knew that it was a natural human reaction to worry. Jesus came to fulfill the law. Jesus came to set a higher standard to the previous way of doing things. Jesus came not just to tell us what to do and what not to do. He came with the POWER to accomplish the law. The people didn't understand it at first. But after Pentecost, the Holy Spirit came to live within the believer, giving each and every person who is IN CHRIST the actual ABILITY not to worry. We CAN do it, BECAUSE WE HAVE THE HOLY SPIRIT!

Philippians 4:6-7 says,

> Be ANXIOUS FOR NOTHING, but in everything by PRAYER AND SUPPLICATION, with THANKSGIVING, let your requests be made known to God; and the peace of God, which surpasses all understanding, will guard your hearts and minds through Christ Jesus. (NKJV)

The Amplified Version of verse 6 says, "Do not fret or have any anxiety about anything...." This is an instruction to the Christian Church from God Himself. God is telling us not to fret or have anxiety about anything, and it is simply NOT okay if we do.

What are we going to do then if we can't worry, gripe, or complain? What does God say? "But in everything (in ALL THINGS) by prayer and supplication, with thanksgiving, let your requests be made known unto God."

So God doesn't just leave us hanging after He tells us not to worry. He tells us what to do. Instead of worrying about something, we are to make the choice to pray about it with thanksgiving. The word "supplication" in Greek means a petition, a specific request. God is right here, right now, giving us a divine remedy for the habit of worry.

So then what happens next? What happens when we choose to replace worry with prayer and thanksgiving? What does God say is the result? "And the peace of God, which surpasses all understanding (beyond all human understanding), will guard your hearts and minds through Christ Jesus."

The Father longs for you to hang out with Him. He longs for your conversation and your companionship. He longs to bear your burdens and carry your load. God takes special pleasure in taking on your cares and worries. He loves you so much, He specifically wrote down in His Word this divine solution. He wants to watch over you and affectionately care for you. I know He does, because His Word says so.

1 Peter 5:7

CASTING THE WHOLE OF YOUR CARE [all your anxieties, all your worries, all your concerns, once and for all] on Him, for He cares for you affectionately and cares about you watchfully. (AMP)

I told you He cares for you. He wants you to be carefree and He wants to carry your load and bear your burdens. God said, "Casting the whole (all of your cares) of your care" on Him.

Notice, we have to do something with the loads; He is not going to take them away from us. WE have to give them to Him. This is something that needs to go on in our individual prayer life. The development of our individual prayer life is the first half of the answer to the worry issue. I can't cast your cares for you; you have to do it. Neither can anyone else cast your cares for you. They are your cares, not mine. They are your cares, not the cares of your best friend, your pastor, or your prayer group. You MUST develop your individual prayer life to the point where it is straightforward and natural for you to pray and thank God rather than worry. You CAN do it, because you have the Holy Spirit as a Helper.

What's the second part of the answer to the worry problem? The answer is found in following two scriptures:

Matthew 11:28-30

Come to Me, all you who labor and are heavy laden, and I WILL GIVE YOU REST. Take My yoke upon you and LEARN FROM ME, for

I am gentle and lowly in heart, and YOU WILL FIND REST for your souls. For My yoke is easy and My burden is light. (NKJV)

2 Peter 1:2

Grace and PEACE BE MULTIPLIED unto you THROUGH THE KNOWLEDGE OF GOD, and of Jesus our Lord.

Can you see that LEARNING OF JESUS and gaining KNOWLEDGE OF GOD through His Word are intimately connected with PEACE AND REST? Peace and rest are the opposite, the reciprocal, of worry. So according to God, the divine recipe for peace and rest is two-fold. FIRST, we are to make a conscious decision to pray with thanksgiving about whatever it is we are tempted to worry about. SECOND, we are to have peace and rest multiplied to us by learning of Jesus and gaining knowledge of God through His Word. It is a two-fold remedy that consists of prayer and reading God's Word. So there is an intimate connection between God's Word and developing an individual prayer life.

Jesus said,

John 15:7

If ye abide in me, and MY WORDS ABIDE IN YOU, ye shall ask what ye will, and it shall be done unto you.

That is precisely why grace and peace are multiplied unto us by the knowledge of God, and why Jesus said if we learn of Him, we will have soul rest. It is all connected. God's Word and prayer. Prayer and God's Word. They are so closely connected and intertwined that they are difficult, if not impossible, to separate.

Some may say, "But you just don't know what I have been through. You just don't know what they said about me. You just don't know how awful I have been treated and what I have been through." No, but I do know my Father, and I know what His Word says. I know my own mountains that were cast into the sea through prayer that were in line with God's Word. I do know these things.

I have a dear friend who calls me often, wanting someone to talk to, telling me all her problems and how insurmountable they are. Have you ever listened to someone get a bit carried away with telling you how bad everything is in their life? Every bit of encouragement you attempt to give that person is met with the piling on of even more grief and burden. Their problems are so great, so intense, and so insurmountable that in actuality there is absolutely nothing you can say or do in the natural that will make them feel better or change their circumstances. Sometimes it seems that such a person can get even more worked up about their problems while talking to you, that their plight even seems worse after they are finished.

So what I do when she calls me and starts to get worked up, I cut her off (kindly, of course) at just about every conversation and say, "Run to God and you will have peace. God is waiting for you with His arms open wide.

"If you stop running from Him by concentrating on your problems instead of the answers…

"If you stop running from Him by rehearsing the worst case scenario instead of believing the best…

"If you stop running from Him by trying to fix your own problems instead of casting the whole of your cares upon Him…

"If you would stop running from God by constantly worrying, fretting, and having anxiety over your circumstances instead of in everything by prayer and supplication make your requests be made know unto Him…

"If you would just stop running from God and run to Him, casting the whole of your cares on him, making your requests known to Him with thanksgiving every time you are tempted to worry, seeking peace through His Word and seeing that peace multiplied unto you through the knowledge of God...."

You know what? At the end of every phone call, she says she feels so much better, and all I basically did was refuse to let her finish talking to me about her problems. I refused to let her get worked up by speaking about the battle instead of the victory. You see, I can't fix her problems, no matter how much I listen and sympathize and hand hold, and no matter what advice I give her in the natural. Her problems are just too great for me to solve, reason through, tell her what course of action to take, what she should say to so-and-so, or what little exercise to carry out. Her tribulations are too great to be comforted by a little anecdote, story, or writing exercise. Nothing will get better and her circumstances will simply not change, no matter what I do for her in the natural.

Now, I can pray for her, and most of the time we spend with people probably would be better spent telling them what the Word of God says, or for praying for them, than hand-holding and sympathizing.

The ONLY One who can help this dear child of God is the Father. He is the only One who can give us peace, not as the world gives us peace, but true peace that surpasses all of human understanding. The Father is the ONLY One who can begin to change circumstances for the better. But to allow our Father to do these things He so yearns to do because He loves us so much, we must run to Him, not away from Him by worrying, fretting, and having anxiety.

We need to develop a private prayer life and constant communion with the Lord. Too many times we resort to prayer only when a great need arises, when we face a crisis of life, or when something bad happens. Then we rush to Him for help. But we really should build such a communion and relationship with Him that He is an ever-present help in time of need.

Too many times prayer has become too formal, scheduled, and reserved just for the times we need God to get us out of a mess. Is He in your life as an unconscious presence at your side with you always? Is prayer a part of your daily routine? Or is prayer only a thing for when a crisis arises?

If your prayer life is going to be effective and produce results, then it must be based upon the Word. This is what I know, and this is how I have received every single major breakthrough in my life. It worked for me because it is God's Word.

I am talking about your individual prayer life. Build a relationship with your Father!!!!! Hang out with your Father!!!! Spend time with your Father!!! Learn what makes Him happy, what pleases Him, how much He loves you, what all He has done for you, and what belongs to you through Christ's redemptive work.

Praise Him, thank Him, build a relationship with your Father, and crave your times together.

It is never too late or too early. Start now, and begin to have His peace guard your heart and mind. Begin to see answers to prayer each and every time you pray. Begin to be a living example of how God watches over His Word to perform it. Begin now to tell others that according to you and your life that God's Word does indeed not return to Him void.

The problem with many people is they try to make God do something, or they try to do something themselves instead of letting God do it. But you can, if you will, just sit back and have fun, lean on God, and see how He gets it done.

A situation arose not too many weeks ago that disturbed me greatly. I met a good friend for lunch and he shared with me some very disturbing news. Along with this disturbing news, he specifically asked for my advice on a matter, because he considered what I had to say as godly counsel. Indeed, I did share with him advice based on the Word of God and he appreciated it. Then I told him that I would pray for him specifically regarding these issues. But I was still disturbed, concerned, and yes, I was still tempted to worry about the issues that we discussed.

About an hour later, during work, during a surgical procedure, I just started laughing out loud, and my assistant asked me what I was laughing about. I told her that I was happy and curious at the same time about how God was going to work this problem out, because I cast that care on Him, and I knew that I knew that I knew that He would work it out to the good.

From that moment on, I never gave it another worrisome thought. Not another concern, not another fret, no more anxiety, because I cast the care on God AND I brought it before Him in prayer and supplication with thanksgiving. And, of course, God came through again, and this issue that was so disturbing is turning out to be a blessing for all involved.

If you're not careful, you can get so involved thinking you have to do it and carry the load. God does not want you to be under any type of load. He wants to carry your load so you can be burden-free. He certainly does not want you to try and carry someone else's load. If you are not careful, you can get so caught up in helping others and showing them love that you begin to take on their burdens and their loads. If you are not careful, this can lead to that person being dependent on you for their happiness. This is not God.

How do you know if your attempts to help someone have gone too far?

If thoughts of that person and their problems begin to weigh heavily on you.

If you begin to have worry, fretting, or anxiety associated with that person's problems.

If you find that your happiness is beginning to depend on whether that other person is happy or not from your help.

God doesn't want us to worry or fret or have anxiety about anything. Now there is a difference between having responsibility and being faithful to your responsibility, and worrying and fretting and stewing. As the owner of my business, I have the responsibility to make decisions and act upon those decisions. I don't just sit back in the face of an issue associated with my business and not fulfill my responsibilities as the boss. But what I do on a very regular basis is, when I am tempted to worry or fret or be overly anxious about something, I cast the care on God and proceed with my actions and decisions in a confident and carefree manner.

For instance, if one of my patients stops breathing during a procedure, I don't just stop what I am doing, sit down at my desk and have a coke, expecting God to supernaturally intervene!!! No, I act on my responsibility as the surgeon to physically intervene with positive pressure oxygen, the administration of drugs, or whatever is needed, and if concern comes my way during this event, I certainly and definitively say a quick prayer and thank God for helping during the situation. THEN, the peace of God comes over me and allows me to operate at maximum efficiency!!!

That is my Father on the throne. My Father sits on the throne!!! God is out to help you and love you, not out to get you. He is your Father. There is a longing in His heart to meet your needs. There is a longing in His heart to bear your burdens. The entire Old and New Testaments lead us to one conclusion, and that is: God longs and loves to answer prayer.

In Jeremiah 33:3 He says,

CALL UNTO ME, AND I WILL ANSWER THEE, and shew thee great and mighty things, which thou knowest not.

So you can readily see how important it is that you learn to fellowship with Him and get to know Him through prayer. You must understand how important it is to learn to pray scripturally. It is more necessary that you learn to pray than anything in life. Education is important, but prayer is more important. It is more important that you learn to pray than it is to be a success in the business world. It is more important that you learn to pray than it is that you learn to be a great singer, politician, or lawyer. It is more important to learn how to communicate with God than it is to know how to be a good parent or spouse. It is simply more important than anything else you could spend your time on.

If you don't know how to pray, then you are at a disadvantage.

The most important thing in the world is to learn how to contact your Father.

The person who does not know how to pray is handicapped in life, because when a great crisis comes, he will not know how to meet it.

If you begin to build a relationship with your Father through prayer, and His Word begins to abide in you, you will begin to find yourself seeking first His Kingdom.

If you begin to build a relationship with your Father through prayer, and His Word begins to abide in you, you will begin to realize His peace surrounding you through the trials of life.

If you begin to build a relationship with your Father through prayer, and His Word begins to abide in you, you will begin to realize all the things being added unto you.

If you begin to build a relationship with your Father through prayer, and His Word begins to abide in you, you will begin to realize the void in your life beginning to fill with the only substance that can fill it—the substance and fragrance of your Father through Christ Jesus.

If you begin to build a relationship with your Father through prayer, and His Word begins to abide in you, you will look up one day, and say, "My life is complete. I am complete in Christ. I am complete through my union with Christ."

Colossians 2:10 says,

> *And you are COMPLETE through your UNION WITH CHRIST. He is the Lord over every ruler and authority in the universe. (NLT)*

> *And you are COMPLETE IN HIM, who is the head of all principality and power. (NKJV)*

What about fear? How destructive is fear? What does God have to say about fear?

A lot of people have different opinions about fear. Many people think that fear is good. Some people think that it is a good motivator. Others think just a little bit of fear is okay some of the time. I must admit that I am really not interested in the opinion of other men. What I want to do is find out what God has to say about fear. I want to find out why God tells us that we must release ourselves from fear. I want to know what God has to say about fear being a roadblock to receiving His blessings through Christ. I want to know why God is so adamant about us not walking in fear.

The Bible calls fear a spirit, which is not from God. Anything that is a spirit and is not from God, personally I want to have nothing to do with it. Second Timothy 1:7 says,

For God has not given us a SPIRIT OF FEAR, but of power and of love and of a sound mind. (NKJV)

What kind of spirit is fear if it is not from God? Fear is a haunting, teasing, tormenting spirit. Fear has torment. First John 4:18 says,

There is NO FEAR IN LOVE; but perfect LOVE CASTETH OUT FEAR: because FEAR HATH TORMENT. He that feareth is not made perfect in love.

God says fear has torment, and God calls fear a spirit that is not from Him. God said He did not give us this spirit of fear; instead He gave us the spirit of love, power, and a sound mind (or sound thinking). When we are in fear, we don't have love (because perfect love casts out fear), power, or sound thinking. When we are in fear, God is telling us that we can't think right!!! I don't have to give you an illustration to make you understand that. We all know that in a state of panic, we are rendered out of sound thinking, for that is exactly what panic is.

A doctor who panics in a life-threatening situation is not thinking correctly or soundly. He forgets what he knows and cannot operate with a sound mind. A pilot who panics in an emergency is rendered useless and cannot think straight. A parent who panics when their child is in danger is useless because they do not have a sound mind. GOD IS TELLING US THAT WHEN WE ARE IN FEAR, WE ARE RENDERED OUT OF SOUND THINKING.

Someone may say, "Yeah, but a little bit of fear is okay, isn't it? I mean, it is only natural to have a little fear."

Let's see if God has more to say about fear. Revelation 21:8 says,

But the FEARFUL, and unbelieving, and the abominable, and murderers, and whoremongers, and sorcerers, and idolaters, and all liars,

SHALL HAVE THEIR PART IN THE LAKE which burneth with fire and brimstone: which is the second death.

Fear is most certainly NOT okay!

A little bit of fear is NOT okay!!

According to God, the first two qualities listed here that will cause a person to inherit hell are the fearful and the unbelieving! If fear is present, then unbelief of God's Word is present! To be fearful, you have to say, "I don't believe what God says in His Word is true." Fear is a roadblock to faith and a roadblock to receiving.

Is a little bit of fear okay?

In response to that question, let me ask...

Is a little bit of adultery okay?

Is a little bit of murder okay?

Is a little bit of unbelief okay?

Is a little bit of the abominable okay?

Is a little bit of whoremongering okay?

Is a little bit of sorcery okay?

Is a little bit of idolatry okay?

Is a little bit of lying okay?

No!! Of course not!! God lists these sins as part of the person who "shall have their part in the lake which burneth with fire and brimstone."

Fear is a spirit. Fear is a thief and a robber. Fear robs people of their destinies. Fear holds people captive. The believer who overcomes is the believer who will not be afraid. The person who will walk on water is the person who has no fear. The man who will not be burned by fire is the man who will give no place to fear. Fear leads to destruction. Fear has torment. Fear takes one to the depth of heartache and destruction. Fear is a spirit. Fear is a roadblock to receiving.

The words "fear not" and "be not afraid" are mentioned over and over and over again in the Bible. Obviously, God is trying to tell us something! He is telling us that we must resist fear. He is telling us that fear is a roadblock to receiving.

Someone may say, "Yeah, but is fear really a bondage? I mean, that is going a bit too far, isn't it?"

Romans 8:15 says,

For you did not receive the SPIRIT OF BONDAGE AGAIN TO FEAR, but you received the Spirit of adoption by whom we cry out, "Abba, Father." (NKJV)

Here God contrasts the spirit of bondage to fear with the Spirit of adoption, or sonship, which is the Holy Spirit.

For those who fear death, God told us,

Hebrews 2:14-15

Inasmuch then as the children have partaken of flesh and blood, He Himself likewise shared in the same, that through death He might destroy him who had the power of death, that is, the devil, and RELEASE THOSE WHO THROUGH FEAR OF DEATH were all their lifetime subject to bondage. (NKJV)

God says that fear will make us subject to bondage!

God calls fear a spirit.

God tells us fear is not from Him.

God tells us that fear will cause us not to think soundly.

God tells us that fear has torment

God contrasts the spirit of fear with the Holy Spirit.

God lists the fearful along with murderers and adulterers.

God is clearly telling us that fear is bad and fear is not okay!!!

Fear is MUY MAL!!! Fear is so bad that it can actually connect us spiritually to the things that we fear! Job actually connected himself to his tragedies through his fears!!

Job 3:25

> *For the thing I GREATLY FEARED has COME UPON ME, and what I DREADED has HAPPENED to me. (NKJV)*

The fear of disease will connect you to the disease that you fear.

The fear of financial lack will connect you to poverty.

The fear of an adulterous relationship will connect you to problems in your marriage.

The fear of tragedy striking your kids will connect you to disaster.

The fear of death will spiritually connect you to death.

Fear is a spiritual connector and operates by the same principles that faith operates by.

Fear is perverted faith.

Fear is faith that the Word of God is not true or will not come true in your life.

Fear is the reciprocal of faith.

Faith comes by hearing and hearing by the Word of God.

Fear comes by hearing and hearing by the Word of the devil.

It is impossible to please God without faith.

It is impossible to please the devil without fear.

Faith is necessary to operate in the Kingdom of God system.

Fear is necessary to operate in the kingdom of darkness.

Faith will bring something out of the unseen realm and make it manifest. Faith is the substance of things hoped for, the evidence of things not seen.

Fear will bring something out of the unseen realm and make it manifest. Fear is the substance of things you hope NOT to happen, and is the evidence of things you continue to see in your past.

Fear is perverted faith.

Fear is faith in the devil.

Fear says, "I really don't believe what the Word of God says is true."

The fear of poverty is really the fear that Philippians 4:19 is not true.

The fear of disease is really the fear that 1 Peter 2:24 is not true.

The fear of bondage is really the fear the Colossians 1:13 is not true.

Fear of tragedy is really the fear that the 91st Psalm is not true.

And here is the deception: Satan wants you to think that fear is okay, that a little fear is okay, and that fear can be a good motivator. All lies!! He wants you to think that fear is okay while he slowly connects you to what you fear, because you have now allowed access to him. You have given the enemy a foothold or an opportunity through your fears.

Fear is NOT a good motivator!! That is a lie, and it is propagated by the father of lies. John 8:44 says,

Ye are of your father the devil, and the lusts of your father ye will do. He was a murderer from the beginning, and abode not in the truth, because there is no truth in him. When he speaketh a lie, he speaketh of his own: for HE IS A LIAR, AND THE FATHER OF IT.

You may see immediate results, or what appears to be immediate results, with motivation by fear; but in reality fear is digging a ditch deeper and deeper into your soul, because it is a spirit and it has torment. Before you know it, walking in fear becomes natural to you, and you get very comfortable with fear in a perverse sort of way. Proverbs 29:25 says,

The FEAR OF MAN BRINGS A SNARE, but whoever trusts in the LORD shall be safe. (NKJV)

Fear is not good in ANY form or for ANY reason.

Fear brings a snare!

Fear brings with it a snare, a trap!

Hebrews 13:6 says,

So that we may BOLDLY SAY, The Lord is my helper, and I WILL NOT FEAR what man shall do unto me.

We are to BOLDLY proclaim our LACK of fear!

We are to BOLDLY proclaim our faith in God, NOT fear of man!

The Lord is our helper!

We will NOT fear what man shall do!

Faith says, "The Lord is my helper!"

Fear says, "Be frightened of your adversaries."

Faith says, "I believe the Word of God is true no matter what the circumstances are!"

Fear says, "God will not come through this time."

Philippians 1:28

And DO NOT [for a moment] BE FRIGHTENED OR INTIMI-DATED in anything by your opponents and adversaries, for such [constancy and fearlessness] will be a clear sign (proof and seal) to them of [their impending] destruction, but [a SURE TOKEN and EVIDENCE] of your DELIVERANCE AND SALVATION, and that from God. (AMP)

According to God, our lack of fear and intimidation is a "sure token" of our deliverance.

According to God, our lack of fear and intimidation is "evidence" of our salvation.

John 14:27

Peace I leave with you, MY PEACE I GIVE TO YOU; not as the world gives do I give to you. LET NOT YOUR HEART BE TROUBLED, NEITHER LET IT BE AFRAID. (NKJV)

Jesus told us NOT to be afraid!

If we fear, we have lost faith in God's Word.

Can you see the overwhelming scriptural evidence of the evil of fear? The Bible tells us that fear is a spirit and it is not from God. The Bible tells us that fear has torment. The Bible lists fearfulness as a sin. The Bible tells us that fear brings a snare. The Bible tells us over and over again to be not afraid. The Bible tells us that fear will make us subject to bondage. The presence of fear in our lives signifies our lack of faith in God's Word. Fear denies the Word of God, and thus cannot be tolerated. Fear is a major roadblock to receiving.

About the Author

Dr. Lloyd Hudson lives in Tulsa, Oklahoma, with his wife Jamie and his three children Morgan, Drew, and Nick. He is a member of First Baptist Church, Tulsa.

Dr. Hudson is a practicing Oral Surgeon and the owner of the Oklahoma Wisdom Teeth Center. He received his Bachelor of Science degree from Baylor University, his Doctor of Dental Surgery degree from Baylor College of Dentistry, and his Medical Degree from the University of Louisville School of Medicine.

His passions include reading and teaching from the Word of God and spending time with his family in their many activities.

Printed in the United States
124861LV00004B/56/P